D0910870

WHO'S GOT YOUR BACK?

Looking To Ourselves, Others, and God

MICHAEL SLATER

TABLE OF CONTENTS

ACKNOWLEDGMENTS

The past year has been a journey into the writing of this book, *Who's Got Your Back?* This book is about coming alongside one another for encouragement and support. Life is challenging and we cannot make it on our own. We need the support of others and know in our hearts that we are not alone. All of this has been played out with truth and meaning in the writing of this book. There have been many involved along the way and I want to take this opportunity to thank all those who have done so much to support and encourage the writing of this book.

To Michael and Diane Stuart. Michael, we met two years ago at a men's conference and a friendship of trust and encouragement developed that weekend. I shared with you my intention of writing this book. You told me of your wife Diane and her gift for editing and proofing documents. We met and I shared with her the thoughts of the book. Diane, you then became part of the writing and proofing of the book. You have been the key person in this whole endeavor. You are so gifted and gracious and your insights and corrections have made the book come together. I know God put you and Michael into my life. Thank you so much—it has been a wonderful experience working with you on all the chapters of the book.

To Chuck Clayton. I came by to see you one morning at your insurance agency. In the course of our conversation I told you about my desire to write the book, *Who's Got Your Back?*, during this coming year. I told you my hope was to find a place that was quiet and where I could be alone to write. You got up from your desk and showed me a vacant office you had next door that you would make available to me. We walked into the office and there was the desk already set up and the quiet office that I had prayed for. I spent one year there writing, outlining, and putting together the book.

It was a wonderful place to go and think, write, and pray. Thank you so much for making this available. This place of retreat and quietness attributed much to the contents of the book. Also, the coffee and donuts on Thursdays were an added blessing and nourishment. Thanks Chuck—like a good neighbor, State Farm was there.

To Ralph Polendo Jr. (You will always be Junior to me) All your gifts of design, layout, and computer talent graciously came alongside of this project. You are such a gifted young man. Thank you for your friendship and commitment to this project and to Stretcher Bearer Ministries. I am so proud of who you are and all you will be in the future. I know God has His hands on your life.

To Bob Hunt, who continued to encourage me in the writing of this book and my ministry. You are a true inspiration to me. I know the Lord has put us back together again for a greater purpose. It will play out Bob.

To Denise Churchill, who began the early editing process with me. Your words of wisdom and support for me and this project in the early stages was so beneficial. I enjoyed all our times of talking over the chapters. Thank you for all your words of encouragement to me.

To Lance and Cindy Cameron. Thank you for so many years of loyalty and belief in me and my ministry. For the past several years you have given me an office—a place to get away, study, and continue to pursue the dreams of this ministry of encouragement and support. You have been so faithful.

To the group of supporters of this project over the past two years—thank you. I will meet and thank each one of you personally and be so excited to give you a copy of the book. Your financial support allowed me many weeks of dedication to the writing of the book.

I also want to thank Ralph and Dorothy Polendo. I value your friendship and belief and support of me and my ministry for so many years. Every other week I receive a personal note of encouragement from you. I have all of them in my desk. It is quite a pile of notes, cards, and letters. I have pulled them out often and reread them at times when I needed encouragement in my own life. You two are such wonderful people. Thanks for your encouragement and friendship.

To my wife Gilda. You are always an encouragement to me and I know you have my back. I love you so very much and am thankful you have been part of my life. You have believed with me in regards to this book. I thank God for all of our years together and for all that are ahead. I know we will continue to love each other and always be there for one another. I know our backs our covered, for we have one another.

— *Mike Slater*

PREFACE

The purpose of this book is to help the reader know that one's back is covered by the three elements: 1) oneself, 2) others, and 3) the Lord. This book is an affirmation of that.

WELL, WHO'S GOT YOUR BACK?

Who's got your back? If someone asked you that question, how would you answer? Does anyone in your life come to mind? If so, would it be a family member, a friend or someone in your church? In your darkest hours, who would come alongside of you with encouragement, support and their presence for you? When you are lonely and afraid, whom can you really count on?

For some who are reading this book, maybe no one comes to mind. You understand the question, but you just can't think of anyone. You know a lot of people, talk to them regularly, and associate with them in some manner, but not at a level of real concern and brotherhood for you.

I'm convinced of two things relating to the question of "Who's got your back?" The first is that many of us do not have or feel the support and concern of others. We're in contact with lots of people, associate with them in family settings, interest groups and even in church. Yet the relationships are not a deep association of concern and involvement with each another.

To illustrate the point, there's a great verse in Proverbs 18:24 that reads, *"There are friends who pretend to be a friend, but there is a friend who stands closer than a brother."* What the writer is trying to express is that in life, we know many people. Yet often times our relationships and friendships tend to lack closeness, understanding, support and concern for others, making it very difficult to establish a truly meaningful relationship.

If I asked you to name ten people who are involved in your life (they can be family members, neighbors, work associates, or people at your church), could come up with ten names? If I offered you a $1000 to come up with ten names, could you do it? (Please don't write and tell me you did it and I owe you a $1,000. I'm just making a point here!) I think it's safe to say that most of us could come up with ten names.

Now, of all the people you listed, who could you turn to for support, prayer and involvement if something happened in your life? Who could you turn to that would be concerned for you, your situation and the challenges you might be facing? Of those people, whom could you really count on? I believe it's safe to say that the list would shrink considerably for most of us.

That's the point the writer of Proverbs 18:24 is trying to get across. We know many people, yet many of us lack friendships that include closeness and support. We tend to label our acquaintances as friends, but friends – real friends – are few and far between. I encourage you to open your Bible to Proverbs 18:24 with a pen in hand. As you read this scripture, whose name would you write in your Bible as that special friend? Who is that friend you could turn to, would care for you and who would have your back? Does a specific name or face come to mind?

One conclusion I've reached is that many of us do not answer to the fullest the true meaning behind the question of "Who's got your back?" I believe the answer should be three fold.

First, we must answer that question as it relates to each of us individually. Each one of us has a responsibility for our self and how we handle life and the challenges before us. We must take some responsibility for our own life. The decisions and choices we make are vital. This is a truth we cannot shortchange.

The book of Philippians happens to be my favorite book in the Bible. I'd encourage you to take the time to read it this week. It's only four chapters, but contains some of the greatest verses and truths concerning our faith and relationship with God. As you read the four chapters, circle the words "I" or "me" each time you see them. You will be amazed the number of times you will come across those two words.

I believe Paul was trying to convey that in life, we must step up, make choices and be responsible in our faith in Christ and challenges in life. Each one of us individually plays a vital role in our personal decisions, determinations and outlook on life. When we think about who has our back, we'd better clearly and soundly make sure that we are covering ourselves.

The following are some verses that address the point I'm trying to make:

"What has happened to me has really served to advance the gospel." —Philippians 1:12

"I eagerly expect and hope that I will in no way be ashamed, but that I will have sufficient courage so that now as always Christ will be exalted in my body." —Philippians 1:20

"For to me, to live is Christ, and to die would be gain." —Philippians. 1:21

"I press on to take hold of that for which Christ Jesus took hold of me." —Philippians 3:12

"I press on toward the goal to win the prize for which God has called me heavenward in Christ Jesus." —Philippians 3:14

"Rejoice in the Lord always. Again I say rejoice." —Philippians 4:4

"I have learned to be content whatever the circumstance." —Philippians 4:12

"I can do all things through Christ who gives me strength." —Philippians 4:13

"And my God will meet all your needs according to His glorious riches in Christ Jesus." —Philippians 4:19

Secondly, when we consider who has our back, we must consider the other people in our life. Those people who come alongside us and are truly concerned for us. Relationships of trust and involvement that give support and strength to each other. People who are looking out for us and willing to be there for us during life's challenges and situations. It's important to know that you are not alone.

What destroys so many people is not necessarily the issue they are dealing with, but rather the feeling that no one is there for them. It can feel like it's them against the world. To be alone can be a terrible, empty, and a hopeless feeling. To wonder if anyone cares about you can be devastating.

To hear someone say, "I'm here for you," can be so uplifting. To know you're not alone can be the strength that enables you to press on and face life's difficult situations and challenges. In sports it is called the home-field advantage. Every sports team desires this advantage of competing on your own field—especially in the playoffs. Hearing and seeing that most of the fans in attendance are cheering for you can be very inspiring. Having all that support gives you the advantage.

When we think about who's got our back, involvement of others is very important. There are just some things that we can't do on our own. We need the assurance that we are not alone. We need to feel secure and know that help and assistance is there for us.

My third and final conclusion is simply God. That's right God. The creator of the heavens, the universe and all there is. The alpha and the omega – the beginning and the end. The King of Kings and Lord of Lords. The great I Am. To be in the presence of God, because God Almighty cares about you. He wants to cover your back.

God cares for us. That's a fact you can take to the bank. God has our backs. He wants to get involved in our lives. He knows, He cares, and He can lighten the load and the burdens.

Simply put, Psalm 23:1 states, *"The Lord is my shepherd."* Those first five words of Psalm 23 give meaning to the 113 words that follow. Belief in the first five words gives meaning and conviction to God and the 113 words that follow. The Lord is *my* shepherd. He is your shepherd—you who are reading this book. God loves you and cares for you. God wants to be part of your life and cover your back.

These three conclusions need to be affirmed within our lives so that we may know the full meaning of having our backs covered. Our personal responsibility, the involvement of others in our lives, and our personal relationship with God, gives true meaning and purpose for having our backs covered. If you answer the question that way, with belief, conviction and certainty, your back will be covered and you will make it!

STAY WITH ME

As you read the chapters that follow, you will have opportunities to look at yourself and reflect on the encouragement you have received. It will also demonstrate the purpose and the importance of believing in yourself, allowing others to come alongside of you, and maintaining a vital, personal relationship with God.

I know you're going to enjoy reading this book and making the journey to help you discover "Who's Got Your Back." I'm praying for each of you reading this book, for those who touch you, and for those you may touch as a result. I'm praying for encouragement and strength in your life as never before. I pray this journey for each of you will be one of encouragement to one another, finding strength in God and discovering purpose within our lives.

May God's blessings be upon each of you!

— Mike Slater

THE BRIEFING

This part of the story of my life takes place in the 1960's. This was the time I went through my teen years and into early manhood. What a time to be a teenager and enter my early 20's. I grew up in an era that has proven to be so memorable, significant and life changing.

The rights of people were spoken and taken to the streets. There were many marches concerning the rights of minorities. Martin Luther King led marches through the south, then to our nation's capitol where his voice proclaimed that memorable "I have a dream" speech which was heard by so many the world over. Change and equality was being proclaimed and realized.

Music would change and have an impact as never before. The British invasion took hold with bands such as The Beatles and The Rolling Stones. It seemed everyone was watching television that historic Sunday night when The Beatles appeared on the Ed Sullivan show. Surf music and The Beach Boys was at its height out here in California and spreading across the country. Folk music carried a different type of meaningful message sung by the likes of Bob Dylan, Joan Baez and Peter, Paul and Mary. The times they were changing.

President Kennedy was assassinated in Dallas, Texas. The following week, the whole country seemed to come to a halt and mourned the loss of our President. Tears flowed freely and we all were part of the memorial service that witnessed a young son saluting his father. How and why did something as awful as this happen?

Cassius Clay became Muhammad Ali and became the new heavyweight champion of the world. He floated like a butterfly and stung like a bee. No sport had seen a personality like that of Ali. UCLA dominated in college basketball under coach John Wooden and won 88 consecutive games. It was a NCAA record. Joe Namath led the New York Jets to win the Super Bowl. He predicated a victory that most thought would never happen. Broadway Joe proved them wrong and his word and promise were fulfilled.

Protests against our involvement in the Vietnam War were taking place everywhere. While the war in Vietnam continued, many young people stood up against it. The peace movement spread. Flower power was real and many cried, "Give peace a chance!" Music and protest came together in a country setting called Woodstock, a festival that took place on a 600-acre dairy farm with 500,000 concertgoers attending. The voice of this generation would not go away.

My high school days were encapsulated in this time period. Basketball was the center of my life. I played hard, enjoyed the competition, and dreamed of one day going to college and playing for John Wooden and the UCLA Bruins. This was also the time when I got my drivers license and my first car. Oh, how I remember that car. It was a 1955 Chevy...Bel Aire. It was a four-door, pink and gray in color. (Pink and gray was very cool in those days, wasn't it?). It had baby moons for hubcaps (I recall that baby moons were also cool at that time...weren't they?). So what if reverse sometimes didn't work. I had my friends to push me backwards, and it was my set of wheels!

Dating and looking for that special girlfriend was high on my agenda. I remember dating and thinking each girl was "the one". I was excited about the possibility of having a girlfriend. There was just one problem...they didn't agree with me. I can't tell you how many times I had my heart broken, but it was part of the game of love.

I loved music, The Beatles, The Rolling Stones, The Doors, Bob Dylan, The Beach Boys and so many others. Music was a vital part of my life. Not only the musical sounds, but the lyrics and meaning that came from so many of the songs. I even formed my own band and dreamed that one day we would be on the main stage performing with all the girls going crazy over us. Like I said, it was a great time for dreaming.

YOU'RE IN THE ARMY

It was in 1969 when something happened that would impact my life like nothing else I had ever experienced. My number came up and I was drafted into the service. The next two years would be spent in the United States Army. One year of my service time would take place in Vietnam, fighting as an infantryman in the war.

This time of service would prove to be most memorable and life changing. I entered a world and experience like nothing I had ever faced or imagined before. I was taken from my comfort zone and a world that I enjoyed. At 20 years of age, I was embarking on a journey and experience that would significantly change my life forever.

From my training and experiences that took place over the next two years, I learned many truths and lessons. These truths and lessons proved to be invaluable and essential to my health and well-being. Much of what I learned still remains with me, even years after my military service came to an end. Those truths and lessons have proven to be as valuable and important to me now as they were during those days of military service.

As I think back on my life in the Army and in the war in Vietnam, I would like to share with you some of the things I learned; things that have helped me deal with this real life situation and have helped me to get through it.

THE THREE T'S

My first seven months in the Army were spent in training; the first 12 weeks in basic training which was followed by 16 weeks of advanced infantry training. The first two weeks proved to be the most difficult. I was placed in a situation totally foreign to me. I was scared, lonely and felt terribly inadequate. I wondered how on earth I could possibly get through not only the first 12 weeks of training, but also all that lay ahead for the next two years.

At night, after some very long days, I would lie in my bunk in the barracks and think about my situation and what I was facing.

I tried to sleep but to no avail. I spent many hours with my head deep in my pillow, wondering, thinking and sometimes crying silently to myself, "God, how am I going to make it?" Though this might seem a little dramatic, it really wasn't. They were the real feelings this 20-year old, as well as countless others, had to face. We were all thinking and feeling pretty much the same.

These beginning moments that turned into weeks and months is where I would learn the importance of what I would call the three T's—Training, Time and Trust. The three T's would be intertwined in all that I learned in the months to come.

First, I learned the vital importance of training. Training hard and long. Learning from others who could impart wisdom and understanding. They had the knowledge that I needed to grasp, and the training that would better equip me for the tasks to come. This would enable me to succeed and accomplish my mission.

During the rest of our training, the most critical lesson we had to learn was how to *best* spend our most fleeting and precious asset—time. There were massive amounts of intense training that had to be accomplished in a quickly decreasing and extremely limited number of training hours, days and weeks. Maintaining and staying on schedule was critical. These periods of time became more and more precious with each passing hour.

We learned that time and training went hand-in-hand and required getting up early, diligently keeping on schedule, and being ever mindful that we had to successfully learn and complete all of the tasks and assignments in this short time. Not only our mission, but also our very lives depended on our ability to effectively manage our time. Obviously, we learned not to waste time, and became committed to it.

Finally, the concept of trust was realized. Trusting the people who trained me, taught me, and imparted wisdom to me. Trust in their knowledge and experience that was beyond my own. Learning to trust in a group of men being formed into a unit of soldiers, committed to one another, and taking on responsibility for each another, was a critical and valuable lesson.

FEARS, WEAKNESSES AND STRENGTHS

I learned in my first seven months of training how to deal with my fears, weaknesses and strengths. Some things came naturally to me and were my strengths; I understood and was able to effectively use what I was being taught. Other things didn't come so easily, and I didn't get them right away. I really struggled and felt these particular things were way beyond my capabilities. I felt there was no way I could achieve what was before me. Those were definitely my weaknesses!

Most of all, I had to admit I was scared and apprehensive. Fear was an emotion that existed within me. I was afraid for my life and myself. I feared the unknown and what I knew I had to face. I feared what I felt were my own limitations. I know men are not supposed to admit it, but here I was, a man and a soldier, and I was afraid at times. One of the most important lessons I learned was to not be ashamed of my weaknesses or fears, but rather to face them and deal with them—to get help and conquer them.

I had to realize that I had all three T's within me. At times, one proved stronger than the others. I learned how to effectively handle and deal with each. I learned to understand how I could merge all three and let all three make me a better person, and I learned how to deal with the situations and tasks that I had to face.

Next, I had to grow in understanding of the enemy, the war and battles that would be fought. This battle and enemy were real. I knew I would have to face them—they were not going to go away. To take the training, the time spent, and the trust that I had learned, meant that defeat was not an option.

LESSONS FROM WAR—STILL APPLICABLE

Years have gone by since I served my country. I no longer wear the uniform, carry the weapon, or walk in a country that was mired in war and its casualties. Those days are gone. So are the times of war and countless battles. I believe I served well and I know I did my best. I was one of the fortunate ones that survived and came home.

To be very honest with you, not many months go by that I do not recall my times of service in the armed forces. I recall them not only for the memories and impact it had on me, but also for the lessons and truths I learned that still apply to my life so many years after.

I'm still working on understanding the past battles and enemies that are still, at times, part of my life. Enemies and battles that want not only to destroy me, but also want to destroy my family and loved ones. Life is challenging and there are many battles that each and every one of us must fight.

I am also still learning to deal with the fears and weaknesses that sometimes creep into my life. They were, and still are, real emotions that affect my thinking. I try to be aware of the strengths I still possess and make every effort to use them wisely. I realize that fear, weakness and strength continue to play a role in my life; challenging who I am, what I will be, and the outcome of so many life choices, decisions, and challenges that are part of my world.

The truth I continue to appreciate and value most is 'time'. Time is the most precious asset in our lives. It is truly a gift. Time is to be used, not wasted. Time with my family should be spent wisely, just as it should be in my work and my relationship with God. It is difficult to realize or understand the purpose time has in our lives, and how quickly it goes by.

THE KEY LESSON – LEARNED AND STILL APPLIED

Of all the lessons I've learned, and all the truths that were taught to me in the military, the one that still remains at the top of the list and holds tremendous value and meaning to me is the commitment *to* and *for* one another. I learned the value of a group of soldiers, molded into a unit of all for one.

In wartime, one person could never win a battle. I was one of many working together as a unit. The support of others was essential. There were Air Force, Navy, Marines, artillery, intelligence, medics, and chopper pilots, among others, all working together in unity with purpose. All were needed by, and had value to one another. All were committed and cared for one another.

What it came down to was the encouragement and support of one for another. We really cared for each other and understood our roles and the value we had to each other. There were many phrases used that expressed what it was truly all about. Phrases like: "I've got your back." "Whose got your back?" "Cover me!" "We are in this together." "We're going to make it!" "We need each other." "Keep alert." "You can count on me!"

These were not tongue-and-cheek statements merely spoken. They were not clichés to make us feel better. They were foundational truths spoken to each other, for each other, lived out with conviction and purpose for survival. These truths were provided to and received by every man there without hesitation even if the provider and receiver didn't know each other personally.

OUR PURPOSE TOGETHER

It's from this background and my experience in the armed forces that lays the foundation and mission of this book, *Who's Got Your Back*. The purpose of *Who's Got Your Back* is a journey for men towards encouragement of one another, strength in God, and achieving purpose in our lives. We are reading this book and enlisting with each other for 12 weeks. The purpose can be summed up as follows:

1. **Encouragement and support of men for each another.** This study should not be done on your own. A group of men is needed to journey together through the study; men committed to the encouragement and well being of others.

2. **Strengthening our relationship with God.** Our world and our families are in desperate need of men of God. Men whose convictions, values and strengths stem from their encounter with the living Christ. An encounter that grows

deeper and deeper each day because of the presence of the Holy Spirit.

3. **The desire to live a life of purpose and victory.** This study will help us find meaning and purpose in our lives and for whom we are; to run the race, fight the good fight and achieve victory; and to feel good about who we are and what we've been through.

We need this study because a battle exists for your marriage, your family, and you. Life is challenging at all ages and phases of life. We cannot make it on our own. We need the support of others and need to know in our hearts that we are not alone. We need to give our lives to God and live within His realm. We need to be men of God.

EIGHT KEYS TO THE JOURNEY

1. **Be committed to the 12 weeks.** Commitment is a powerful and positive word. It is a word of loyalty and priority. Give yourself to this study until completion. Do not try it for just a week or two. Each week builds upon itself. All 12 weeks are needed for completion and achieving positive results.

2. **Be real and honest.** As you share with one another in the group, be open and honest. Do not fake it or hide behind a mask. One thing you need to realize is that most of us are very similar in nature and in life's challenges. You are not that unusual or unique. Others will likely relate to you. Also, by opening up, you will help others to feel at ease about themselves and sharing.

3. **Be attentive to one another.** Really listen and tune in to one another. Listening is something that we may have to learn how to do. We can all hear, but listening is something far deeper and much more important.

4. **Do not waste time.** I can't stress enough how important time is to achieving success. The two hours you spend

together each week is not that long, yet can be very positive and powerful. Use the time you spend together to its fullest. Stay focused on the purpose of your being together. Talk about sports and politics some other time.

5. **Respond through action.** Get involved with others. Talk to each other. Encourage one another and help someone. Give of yourself to others where possible. Let them know you are listening, concerned and willing to get involved.

6. **Have and Use Your Bible.** Let the word of God be used among your group. Seek out the Word and let it speak to the situations and challenges that arise within your group. Trust in the word of God to give wisdom, light and guidance to each one of you. Speak and use the Word to each one gathered.

7. **Be on time.** Be considerate and courteous to one another. If you agree to meet and start at 7:00, then by all means, keep that commitment. Don't make others wait on you. Value and respect each other's time and commitments.

8. **Uplift and pray for each other.** One of the most important responsibilities we have as Christians is the privilege of praying for one another. Take these men and their stories; the words they speak and issues they are dealing with, before the Lord. Let them know you are praying for them. This sense of caring goes on even after the meeting adjourns. Prayer binds us to God and to one another.

LET'S SIGN UP

What do you think? Are you ready to sign up? I know this time together will encourage, challenge, and benefit each one of you.

Be in prayer for yourself. Be in prayer for your friends. Be in prayer for the teachings within the book. Enjoy this time together. Take the opportunity to make new friends. And most of all, take this opportunity to grow nearer to God.

Whether or not you are part of a small group, Bible study group, or life group, I hope this book will inspire you personally. If you are not part of a small group, I hope you may be encouraged enough to seek out or possibly establish one.

We are going to make it! My prayers are with you and your small groups. *I've got your back!*

— **Pastor Mike**

CHAPTER ONE

WHO'S GOT YOUR BACK?

Let me present you with four powerful words—four words that most people have heard at least once—a phrase that is said to offer support, comfort, and security. Stop and think about where you might have heard the words "I've got your back." Was it in a movie? On television? Did you say it to someone or did someone say it to you? Four words, when presented to someone, require a commitment. Four words, when accepted, give relief to the situation.

I wish I could claim to be the one who came up with this phrase. I don't even know when or where it began, who first said it, or what the context was at the time. It's one of those phrases that has been around for a long time. These four words are powerful, meaningful, and so needed by all of us. These four words, when said together, hold so much truth, encouragement and confidence for all.

TONY THE BARBER

Tony the barber is a good friend of mine. We've known each other for over 25 years. We've shared so much, supported one another, and took our time and resources to give to each other. Tony is a good man who loves the Lord and loves his family.

Over the years we have grown further apart in distance, since we no longer live in the same city. However, we continue to call each other, have lunches together, and uphold each other in prayer. Recently, during the same time period as the writing of this book, something happened to Tony. It's amazing to me to realize how this incident, as well as what Tony said, had a place in the meaning and purpose of this book.

It was a Monday morning. Tony got dressed and went outside to pull his truck around to take his children to school. As he walked in the cold towards his truck, he felt peculiar and light headed. He drove the truck to the front of the house and stepped out, fainted, and fell to the ground.

Moments later, Tony's son, Brandon, stepped outside of the house and noticed his dad lying on the ground. He ran to his father and gently rolled him over, noticing his nose had a gash on it and his head was cut. Tony was pale and dazed. Brandon frantically called out to his mother. She came running out of the house and saw her husband on the ground with blood on his face. Not knowing the extent of his injuries, they called 911.

Tony was rushed to the hospital emergency room where the doctors on duty began to work on him. He was attached to various monitors, and a number of tests were being performed to help diagnose his condition. It wasn't long before the readings indicated that his heart was pumping too slowly. As the doctors shared the news of their findings with the family, Tony went into cardiac arrest. A moment later, he flatlined. During the next hour, Tony flatlined three more times. His heart rate was very irregular and Tony's life was in danger.

He was immediately rushed into surgery. A temporary pacemaker was implanted in his chest to regulate his heartbeat. About an hour later, the family received word that the temporary pacemaker was working and that Tony's condition was stable. Though this was good news, it was also determined that he would have to be transported to another hospital where a permanent pacemaker would be implanted.

It was during this time that the family called me and informed me of what had happened to Tony. Since I was traveling out of state, I was physically unable to be with the family. During the hours that followed, I kept in telephone contact with the family. My wife and I took Tony and his family to prayer. When I received the news that Tony was stable and the procedure had been successful, I rejoiced with the family and breathed a big sigh of relief and thankfulness.

It was three days later when I finally spoke to Tony. He had been transferred by ambulance to Kaiser Hospital. For two days we talked and prayed as Tony waited for the next corrective heart procedure. It was during these special telephone conversations that Tony shared so honestly with me his feelings and thoughts of what had happened to him.

During one particular conversation, Tony said to me, "Mike, I really thought my time had come! I got a glimpse of heaven! This was a journey where I was leaving my wife and children. Mike, it scared me. I've *never* felt like that before!"

As Tony was speaking, he began to cry and choke up. I felt his pain, fear and deep concern for his medical condition. I listened intently as he described all that had happened to him the past week. My heart went out to my friend.

I let him know that my prayers had been with him and would continue through his next procedure. I would pray for the heart surgeon who would perform the surgery. I would pray for the team that would assist the surgeon. I would pray for their wisdom and the touch of God during the operation. I tried to convey words and thoughts of comfort, hope and encouragement.

The day of the procedure, a scripture came to mind, which I shared with Tony. It was the 23rd Psalm. I asked him to recite it as he prepared for the procedure. I encouraged him to say it over and over to himself as they wheel him into the operating room. With love and sincerity, I told him, "Let the words of this wonderful scripture speak to you of God's presence, love and concern for you. Somewhere within the phrases of this Psalm, God will speak to you and His peace and presence will draw close to you."

I then prayed for Tony. We joined together as two friends, caring, encouraging and involved with one another. My prayer was for my dear friend who had one more hurdle to jump concerning his health and recovery. Even though we were miles apart, we were together as one in prayer and encouragement for one another. There was no distance between us because of our relationship to God and to each other.

Tony went into surgery. The family gathered in the waiting room, anxious as the time of the procedure began to tick away.

Two hours later his family received the news from the surgeon that all went well. The permanent pacemaker was implanted and the heart was back to a perfect rhythm. Tony was released from the hospital a few days later. What a day of rejoicing and thankfulness to God!

JUST A GLIMPSE OF HEAVEN—WHAT A JOURNEY

A few days after arriving home, Tony gave me a call. He told me he wanted to share with me the thoughts he had just before they wheeled him off to the operating room. He then proceeded to tell me the following story:

"As I lay in bed waiting for them to come for me, I thought of you and the words we had spoken yesterday. Those words gave me encouragement and hope. I went to prayer quoting the 23rd Psalm and praying to God. It gave me confidence. I began to think, Pastor Mike has my back. I am not alone. I put my hand over my heart and said, Lord you have my heart."

"My friend has my back, and God, you have my heart. The peace and presence of God was with me. I had the words, thoughts, scripture and presence of hope within me. I was going to be fine."

The words Tony spoke to me that afternoon touched my heart. To be used in someone's life to encourage and lift up is such a wonderful feeling. I am so thankful that I was able to be there for Tony and his family, even though I couldn't be there physically.

Tony called me one afternoon as I was writing this book about Who's Got Your Back. He knew nothing of this project. When he made the comment that someone had his back, I was given much food for thought. He spoke about everything I was writing about. There are times when we need others to be there for us. Sometimes we need to feel the support, presence and concern for us. It confirmed within me, the need and my desire to keep writing so I could get this truth and book out to the people.

The following week I received a note from Tony:

"Michael,

JUST A GLIMPSE OF HEAVEN—WHAT A JOURNEY.

Thank you for being there always, for carrying my stretcher, and for talking me through the waters and keeping my eyes on Him. Here is a little something...gas is high today. (Enclosed was a small amount of cash.)

Love your friend,

Tony the Barber"

THE MEANING OF "WHOSE GOT YOUR BACK?"

These four words, spoken as a phrase, hold a tremendous amount of truth and power. I am convinced that many have heard this phrase, yet have not grasped the full meaning and purpose behind it. I'd like to break down the phrase and define what these four words truly mean. My prayer is that the depth of their meaning will impact you and your study group.

1. **You are not alone.** What destroys so many people is not necessarily the issue they are dealing with, but the feeling that no one is there for them. It can feel like them against the world. To be alone can be a terrible, empty, and hopeless feeling. To wonder if anyone cares about you must be devastating.

   To hear someone say, "I'm here for you", can be so uplifting. To know you are not alone can be a strength that enables one to continue to press on and deal with difficult situations and challenges. In sports it is called "the home field advantage". Every sports team desires this advantage in the playoffs. That advantage is specific to playing the competition on your home field. Hearing and seeing that most of the fans in attendance are cheering for you can be very inspiring. It's like having an additional player on the field. It gives you the advantage.

2. **I am aware of your situation.** I listened to you and I heard you. My focus and attention were on you. What you said truly mattered. As you took the time to be honest and open, I took the time to listen. Now I have understanding.

3. **I'm looking out for you.** You matter to me and I'm concerned about you. You and your situation are important to me. I am now willing to get involved. What matters to you, matters to me. You can count on me. I am here. I'm committed to you.

4. **I will get involved.** This is such an important message. It has to be conveyed in such a way that people are not afraid to "get involved." People value their time and are not often accepting of the proposal of giving it to others. We need to realize how important and beneficial it is to get involved, and the value of time spent together.

   "I will get involved" means that I am willing to give of myself to you. I will share my strengths, my assets, and my time. I am adding to you and your situation. The addition of myself and some of my resources will be a plus to you, not a negative or liability. My involvement will benefit you and be of assistance.

5. **I will let you know I am here.** During the days and weeks that follow, I will let you know and reaffirm my concern and involvement with you. I will respond to you. You will know for sure that you can count on me because I will make that evident. I will accomplish this by telephone, letter, e-mail, text message, or in person.

   It is important to reaffirm our commitment to one another, and not just during the regularly scheduled meeting times each week. These times of letting a person sense you are thinking of them and are concerned about them can be a tremendous lift and strength as they continue to journey through their situation. Stay in contact with each other.

6. **You have some assurance.** Hopefully, all I'm doing is giving you some assurance and peace of mind. It's a nice feeling

knowing someone is there that is concerned about you. As someone once said to me, "It's nice having someone to talk to, even to shout at. It gives me some peace of mind."

7. **I am praying for you.** This is not just a Christian cliché. What a wonderful thought to know someone is praying for you. You are being lifted up to the Lord in prayer throughout the week. Talk about someone having your back! This prayer is not just for the person being prayed for, but also for you and your involvement with them. Prayer will give you wisdom, insight, hope, and the feeling of God's presence.

8. **Take it on.** That's right! It is an attitude and a feeling inside that I am going to make it. I will pass through this valley. It's like a sport's team putting all their hands together and shouting, "Let's win, we can do it!" I'm beginning to believe that I can triumph. No retreat, no surrender.

9. **Same right back at you.** For all that you are doing for me, I want to give it right back to you. It's all for one and one for all. I want to offer to you all that I have received in my life that has been so beneficial. Each one of us needs to give and receive. Thank you for giving to me. I in return, want to give to you.

WHAT ABOUT US?

Think about personal applications for the group.

1. What comes to your mind when you hear the term, "Whose got your back?"

2. How can we partner with each other?

3. How can we be an encouragement to one another?

4. How can we truly be aware of each other's situations?

5. We are looking out for each other. How can we express that and make it known?

6. I will let you know that I am here for you. How can we be an encouragement to each other in the weeks to come, not just during our meeting times?

7. I am praying for you. How can we integrate prayer in our support of each other?

8. Let's join hands and make a 12-week commitment to one another. Let's close in prayer for our group, and for each of us.

CHAPTER TWO

DEALING WITH FEARS & ADMITTING WEAKNESSES

It was late in the evening and I was seated on a Greyhound Bus traveling up the coast from Los Angeles towards Monterey, California. On that bus were 60 men who were put together for the first time. They had never encountered each other before this day. What brought them together was the destination of that bus.

The bus was traveling to Fort Ord, an army base outside of Monterey, California. All 60 aboard that bus were destined to become part of the armed forces for the next two to three years.

As I sat there looking out the window, the bus rolled on, mile after mile. As we traveled up the highway, I looked upon rolling hills, the ocean, and the lights of the various cities. All were familiar to me since I had traveled this highway many times before.

I recalled the many vacations with my family and friends. Countless days spent at the beaches that are so beautiful along the California coast. There were many moments during the past 10 years of my life that took me along this highway. As I went back in time and reminisced, there was a peaceful smile on my face, for this highway and its memories had served me well.

But this evening, the travel on this highway was like none I had ever taken before. My travel had nothing to do with family, friends or vacations. My destination this evening was an army base. Little did I know all that was to come and all I would encounter during the next two years of my life.

My time in the army and fighting in Vietnam would bring two issues to the forefront that would have to be addressed. It was not so much the training I would go through, the thought of facing the enemy, or even the war. The issues I would encounter would be dealing with my fears and my weaknesses. These would become the two most vital issues I would ever have to admit to and deal with.

When we arrived at Fort Ord, we were ushered into an auditorium. It was late at night, or should I say very early in the morning—about 1:00 a.m. We were told to rest and try to get some sleep. Our beds that night would be one or two of the chairs scattered within the auditorium. Everyone took the advice that was given and spread out as best as they could and tried to catch a few hours of sleep.

I remember sitting in a chair with my head to the side, trying to sleep. I kept opening my eyes and looking around the auditorium that was filled with 300 men. I scanned the many faces that filled the auditorium, yet it felt like I was the only one there. I felt so alone. Everything about this setting felt unfamiliar, unfriendly and empty. This was the feeling that surrounded me that evening as I closed my eyes and tried to get a bit of sleep.

WAKE UP

The following story has impacted various aspects of my life so much that you might be reminded of it again in a later chapter. Not only does this story affect my concept of time, but it also affects my concept of fear!

At 5 a.m. we were awakened, assembled, and taken for some breakfast. The breakfast was not at all like mom would make. It was just some food and some coffee, and it had to be accepted as edible food and drink. After breakfast we were marched over to a supply building where we were issued our army gear that we put into duffle bags.

We then boarded four large flatbed trucks. Approximately 100 men were squeezed into and seated in each truck. We sat alongside each other just like cattle. The trucks drove us to our barracks, which would be our home for the next 12 weeks. This is where we would be assigned to a company and a platoon for our basic training.

When we reached our destination, a Drill Sergeant met each truck. One of them came to the back of my truck and in a brusque tone with words that were not the nicest shouted, "Welcome to your home for the next 12 weeks. You have exactly one minute to get out of that truck and stand in formation. I have just used up 15 seconds of your time. That leaves you less than one minute. Let's Go!"

To be honest with you, the tone of his voice, the tenor of his words, and the look on his face scared the living daylights out of me. He looked so mean...and he was wearing one of *our* uniforms. This was my introduction to fear, which became part of my being.

I had never seen so many men move so fast. They were exiting the truck where exits didn't exist. Duffle bags were flying in every direction. Men were jumping out of and climbing down the truck. I am happy to report that it *can* be done. All 100 men were able to get out of that truck and into formation in record time. It's amazing how fear can motivate people at times.

Those first 30 days of my training were some of the toughest days I had ever experienced. Even though I was there among so many, I felt so alone at times. I also began to feel very inadequate about who I was and what my capabilities were. After lights out, there were times when I would lay in my bunk for hours, unable to sleep. Sometimes I lay there frightened; afraid as a person, afraid as a man, afraid of my tomorrow, and terrified of my future.

There were moments when tears came to my eyes and I hoped no one would notice. I cried silently to myself. I longed to be home, back in a setting that I knew and felt comfortable in. I wanted to be home with my mom and dad, with my brother and my friends. I wanted to be home, sleeping in my own bed.

There were evenings when my bunk became a symbol of my reality and much of what I was feeling inside. I was not going home. Not today, anyway. I was not going to sleep in my own bed. Not tonight or tomorrow. For the next two years, this was my reality and the world that I had to deal with. I would have to train, learn, grow stronger and deal with this situation, no matter how fearful or inadequate I felt.

LOOKING BACK ON LIFE

As I look back on my life, fear and weakness have always been part of my journey.

This probably holds true for you as well. I think fear and weakness are a part of everyone's life. We all go through situations, circumstances and challenges that are beyond our comfort zone and capabilities. We like to rely on our strengths to feel comfortable and at ease within our world. But there are moments in life that don't play out that way.

There are times when we are afraid and we wonder. There are times we feel helpless and hopeless. Is this ever going to get better? How am I going to get through this? How can I meet this challenge and make it? We all have our stories. Often times we do not want to admit it or are ashamed to fess up. Fear and weakness are two feelings that many of us do not want to admit to. They seem to be negative and ugly words that hold little meaning or worth for each one of us.

I can look back on my life and admit that fear and weakness was a significant part of my world. I know I didn't always handle them properly, and unfortunately they did get the best of me at times. I wasn't really schooled on how to handle fear and weakness. So many times they molded me into someone I did not want to be.

LITTLE LEAGUE—NOT FOR ME

In my early childhood, I loved baseball. I always watched it on television and dreamed of playing baseball one day. I grew up in Brooklyn, New York, and my favorite team was the New York Yankees. I knew all the players by name, their positions on the field and their statistics. I dreamed that one day I would be putting on the uniform and the fans would know my name.

When I was 10, we moved to Los Angeles, California. My love for baseball followed me. Then I became a Dodger fan because they moved from Brooklyn to California. I continued to follow the game and really wanted to play the game for myself. But I never did play baseball. I'd like to share with you the reason why.

I used to spend much of my time playing in the back of the apartments where I lived. There was a cement driveway with some garages and a brick wall that separated our apartment from the others. With chalk, I drew a picture of home plate in front of the brick wall. On the wall I outlined where the batter's box would be. Then I walked 50 feet from the batters box and made the pitcher's mound.

Day after day, I would spend hours out there pitching a tennis ball against that wall. I was the pitcher facing batter after batter. I imagined game situations where the bases might be loaded and I had to get a strikeout. A 'walk' would cost the team the game. I would pitch inning after inning, striking out people and imagining them, at times, getting a hit off of me. I developed three pitches. My fastball, change up, and curve. Over the years I got better and better. I could hit tight spots near home plate when I pitched. I could control the spot and placement of the ball more consistently. If I wanted it pitched inside, I imagined it, let the ball go, and many times it arrived right where I wanted it to be placed.

For a young kid, I really was pretty good, now that I think about it. For so many days, weeks and months, I was the pitcher. I was the pitcher, pitching in front of thousands of people in my backyard. In my fantasy world, I was getting the cheers and becoming better and better at my sport. I could cut the corner of the plate with a pitch. Put pressure on me to get the batter out, and I succeeded. I could hear the crowd cheer for me.

From months and months of playing fantasy baseball, I became better at the sport. I could see my improvement from all the games I had played in my backyard. I truly was a good pitcher. I wish you could have been there with me. I believe you would have been impressed. You would have been cheering for me with all the others that I heard so clearly in my backyard.

When I turned 11, my friend who played little league baseball encouraged me to try out for the new season that would
start that spring. I gave it some thought and went to one tryout
session. After that one tryout, I never went back to continue the
process of trying out for the team. It wasn't so much because
I thought I wasn't capable or talented enough. I was aware of
the talent and skill I possessed because I practiced long and hard
against that wall. But I was a young kid, and I was scared. I was
so scared inside that I let it get to me.

I was afraid of the hard ball. It was not a malleable tennis
ball, the ball I felt comfortable with that was so much part of my
athletic ability. Additionally, I would be playing against real kids
my age. Young people who were not a fantasy and could actually hit my pitching. They could show me up and get the best
of me. Most importantly, I could make mistakes in front of real
people. I never made mistakes in front of the fantasy crowd. All
this made me so vulnerable and fearful inside. The strengths that
I had felt for the game had now turned into weakness and fear.

This might sound foolish or silly to you. But the fear I felt
was so real that it had an impact on my little league days (or
absence from) then and into my future. I could not get over my
fears and weaknesses. They were so real to me. I talked to no
one about them. I never played little league. I talked myself out
of it and ruined any chance I had to play. I went to the games
and watched my friend play. I continued to pitch in my fantasy
world in my backyard for another year until we moved.

That way of thinking became so much a part of Mike Slater.
For the years that followed, I was a young person who could
not get over my weaknesses and fears in life's situations such
as sports, school, or within social realms. The challenges of life
were always there. While growing up, fear and weakness often
got the best of me. Many times I talked myself out of things.
Fear and weakness controlled and molded so much of my thinking and its outcome.

I could tell you stories that would fill up pages in this book.
Stories I wish I could relive. I believe the outcomes could have

been different if only I could have controlled the fear and thoughts of weakness that played into my thinking and decision-making process.

THE CHALLENGE OF THE ARMY

Interestingly, the stories and challenges continued in my life. They were not just part of my youth. Now here I was at the age of 20, facing some of the most difficult and challenging events of my life. I was in the United States Army, training to be a soldier and having to do things I had never done, or even thought of before.

I realized during those first 30 days that it was not the training that bothered me. Nor was it the thought of going to war in a country I was not familiar with. It wasn't even the uncertainty of how we would be molded into soldiers, capable of fighting and being victorious. What kept me up at night and what I kept thinking about over and over were my fears and weaknesses in everything that I had to face and all the things that lay ahead for the next two years. I wanted to go home. I wanted to duplicate my little league cop-out, which was, "This just isn't for me." But it was too late. I couldn't!

JOSHUA—MOSES IS DEAD

There is a great man in the Old Testament named Joshua. Recorded in Joshua 1, is an honest and real story of Joshua and his reaction to some news that he would have to face. It can speak to many of us today. It reads as follows:

> "After the death of Moses the servant of the Lord, the Lord said to Joshua, Moses' aide: Moses my servant is dead. Now then, you and all these people, get ready to cross the Jordan River into the land I am about to give to the Israelites. I will give you every place where you set your foot, as I promised Moses. Your territory will extend from the desert to Lebanon and from the great river, the Euphrates, to the Great Sea on the west. No

one will be able to stand up against you all the days of your life. As I was with Moses, so I will be with you; I will never leave you nor forsake you.

Be strong and courageous, because you will lead these people to inherit the land I swore to their fore-fathers to give them. Be strong and very courageous. Be careful to obey all the law my servant Moses gave you; do not turn from it to the right or to the left, that you may be successful wherever you go. Do not let this Book of the Law depart from your mouth; meditate on it day and night, so that you may be careful to do everything written in it. Then you will be prosperous and successful. Have I not commanded you? Be strong and courageous. Do not be terrified; do not be discour-aged, for the Lord your God will be with you wherever you go."

The interesting concept in this story of Joshua is his response and the way he handled this real life situation, whether he liked it or not. Joshua was second fiddle to Moses. He didn't mind that and was comfortable and very content being second fiddle. He probably said, "Moses can be number one. That is definitely okay with me. The people are behind Moses as the leader. He is closest to God, and the Hollywood movie studios will probably make a movie of Moses and not me. The people have confidence and hope in Moses and his leadership ability. I am fine with all of that."

Then one day, the word of the Lord comes to Joshua and declares, "Moses is dead. He is gone and you are now the man in charge to lead the people. You are to step up and take over his leadership." His immediate response is, "No way! I love being second fiddle. Moses was cut out for this. I don't have his tal-ents and I'm not built like him. My speaking ability in front of people is lousy. I'm really not cut out to be number one. Please choose someone else. Thank you, but no thanks."

The struggle is within Joshua, and what lies ahead for him. What is dominating the struggle and his decisions is his sense of weakness and fear. He is fearful within himself and feels totally inadequate to step up and be the leader of these people.

During this conversation with the Lord, there is a phrase that is repeated three times, "Be strong and be courageous." Joshua is also told over and over again not to be discouraged or terrified.

There it is in a nutshell, the issues that are truly affecting Joshua and his future. He is scared and feels inadequate. He has to be strong and courageous to his challenge in life, but also to his fears and weaknesses. He needs to confront his feelings about himself. If he doesn't deal with these issues of fear and weakness, the outcome will not turn out like it should.

What about us? Have we ever felt like Joshua in a situation that was presented to us? Have we ever felt scared, discouraged and weak? Have we ever wished it would just go away, or have we ever tried to talk ourselves out of it?

PLAYING BASKETBALL

When I was in high school, I played basketball. My love for baseball was transferred to basketball. I loved that game! I loved playing it, and I loved watching it on television. My favorite teams were the Los Angeles Lakers and the U.C.L.A. college team coached by John Wooden. I played on my high school basketball team every year, starting with junior varsity and working my way up to varsity.

When I started, I was good, but not great. I played each year, and each year I improved my game. My parents would come out on game days to sit in the stands and watch me play. I can't think of a better feeling than to have your parents cheering for you and being so proud. I always knew where they were seated.

Our team was good, but not great. Sort of like me. We finished fourth in our division out of eight. When I graduated from high school, I went to a Christian college called Biola. The reason I went there was because my best friend went there, and we wanted to go to college together. After being there a month, I tried out for the basketball team. Just trying out was a big step for me. I had never played at this level of competition before.

I played hard and practiced hard for three weeks of tryouts. I did my best, day after day, through all of the tryouts. It was near the end of the third week when a thought continued to play over and over again in my mind. The guys I was competing against for a position on the team were really good. In fact, many were a lot better than me no matter how hard I tried. You could actually call some of them great! This truly was a whole different level of competitive skills and capabilities.

As I continued to practice and observe, I realized that there were *eight* of us trying out for *two* guard positions. In a basketball game, there are only five people who start the game; two guards, two forwards and a center. The rest of the team, usually 10 additional people, are seated on the bench to substitute in and play some when the great players get tired, hurt, or when their playing will make no difference in the outcome of the game.

Throughout my high school days, whether junior varsity or varsity, I always ended up starting. I never was a player coming off the bench. I was always one of the two guards to take the court. That made me feel good and became part of my life all through my high school days of playing basketball. Now, here I was in college, trying to play basketball, realizing there were a lot of guys out there, way better than me. There was no way I was going to start, much less make the team. Out of the eight guards, I saw my self as number six in the rankings. That was not a good position to be in. That meant that for the first time, I would not take the court as a starter.

In my room that evening, I contemplated this situation. I played it over and over again in my mind, always with the same outcome. So many of these guys were better than me that I wasn't going to be a starter anymore. In fact, for the first time, I might not even be good enough to make the team.

All of these thoughts were getting to me. I felt weak, discouraged and ready to give up. I felt like a loser. I couldn't handle what I was feeling, neither physically nor mentally.

I went to the coach the next day and asked if I could speak with him after practice. Later that afternoon, we walked to the side of the gym and sat on the bleachers. I told the coach how much I loved playing basketball and how I enjoyed trying out for the team. I confessed to him that I was here at the college without the help of any kind of scholarship or financial aid. The tuition was not something my parents could afford. I needed to get a part-time job that would allow me to stay at this college and pay my tuition. That would mean I couldn't be on the team. I explained that I couldn't possibly work, study, and practice sports, and be good at any of them. I would have to drop out of the tryouts.

He looked at me and said, "Mike, I understand where you're coming from. Your college tuition is something that has to be addressed. You are a good ball player with a lot of potential. I want you to try out for the team again next year." I remember looking him straight in the eyes and saying, " I will be back, coach. I love basketball and would love to play at this college under your coaching."

We shook hands, then I walked across the court towards the locker room to change. As I walked off the court that day, I knew I wasn't coming back. The issue wasn't so much the money for my tuition, even though there was some truth behind it. The truth is, I felt inadequate as a person. I felt weak and not strong. I was scared and not courageous.

I never walked back on the court again. My basketball days were finished. I never heard the fans cheer again. I never warmed up with the team again, or looked up in the stands to see my mom and dad sitting there. I never again saw my dad wink at me as I ran by during warm up to let me know he believed in me and wished me all the best. I never ran on the court again. Fear and weakness got the best of me.

Now, two years later, I was again challenged by another important life-changing situation. At the age of 20, I was looking at my future for the next two years as a soldier in the army. Right in front of me, once again, were those two ugly and powerful words that would again have to be played out; fear and weakness.

HANDLING FEAR AND WEAKNESS

Now, consider the life you have lived. Are there stories you could share? Are you going through situations (future stories) right now in your personal life, maybe with your family, your finances or your job? Are you facing any challenges today? Do you ever find yourself doing a lot of personal thinking while driving your car? What about when you go to bed. Do you fall asleep right away or do you think, reflect, and contemplate while staring into the darkness, wondering?

Sensing fear and/or weakness can work for you or against you. Fear can paralyze you. It can keep you from moving forward and progressing. It can freeze you from action. Fear can terrify you and play on your thoughts and emotions. It can make you withdraw from fully experiencing the goodness and joy of life. Fear can be the reason you never play little league baseball, college basketball, or participate in a number of other great endeavors in life.

Fear and weakness can and will cause you to doubt. It will cause you to doubt yourself, your purpose in life, and your future. Doubting renders you unable to see clearly. It's like you are in a daze or fog and there is no way out. Then fear steps in and causes you to withdraw and want to escape. It becomes a harmful self-defense (actually self-destructive) mechanism that is not good for anyone.

All in all, fear and weakness are twins that show no mercy, especially if you allow them to rule you or the situations causing you to feel fearful and weak. It doesn't have to be like this. Fear and weakness can work for us if we understand the positive aspects of them and learn how to apply them in our life. We just need to learn how to handle them.

In moderation, these two emotions can motivate us towards self-preservation and creativity. In excess, they are devastating to the human personality. They can threaten our inner peace and outward poise. Dealing with fear and weakness can secure our own liberation from self-defeat. It has been said that fear can save your life or ruin it.

Fear and weakness should make one think. They should produce a determination for betterment within a person. They can be used to help us experience the goodness and joy of our life. Now I will give you some practical advice and suggestions on handling fear and weakness. I hope this insight will inspire you and help provide a positive outcome for your future.

FEAR BUSTERS

First, you need to face your fears. Don't run from them. Here is a great quote from Eleanor Roosevelt, "You gain strength, courage and confidence by every experience in which you stop to look fear in the face."

Think for a moment about the fears and weaknesses that have played a part in your life. Stop right now and look them in the face. What is fear trying to say to you? Are the words and thoughts a lie? What is it saying about you and your actions? Look fear right in the face and assess what is taking place within you, but don't let fear win.

Secondly, admit you are afraid and possibly weak as it relates to something specific you are dealing with. We are not always strong and brave. We are not super heroes. We all have fears and weaknesses. Even the best baseball players strike out sometimes. They don't always get a hit. Get that burden off your chest. Say it out loud right now, "I am fearful and maybe feel a little weak and worn out."

Third, realize that fear can help us see clearly and help us prepare for a necessary undertaking. It can reveal an assessment of a situation that we might not want to admit, but that needs to be addressed. An example might be an athletic competition. Maybe the opponents frighten us or intimidate us because they are stronger in some areas. Instead of being scared and throwing in the towel, use this fear to help you win. Prepare harder to neutralize their strength. We must work harder to counter the other team. If we just give in, we lose even before the game begins.

Fourth, look fear in the eyes and show courage. That's right, courage. Courage is a powerful and positive word of action and determination. You can also call it bravery, guts, nerve, true grit, backbone, or inner strength. It has many nicknames and they all mean the same thing. Courage is the determination to persevere. Remember what was said to Joshua three times after he heard that Moses was dead and he was to become the leader of Israel? He was told to be strong and courageous. Be strong and courageous. Be strong and courageous. Now get that thought in your head and face your doubts and fears.

Fifth, we need to endure. Run that race and fight that good fight. There will be no retreat, and there will be no surrender. It might take a while to conquer the challenges in your life, but you will endure. Give it your best.

Do you remember the first Rocky movie? Rocky goes against the world heavyweight champion in a fight. He's the underdog like none has ever been. He trains hard and the day of the fight comes. The fight is supposed to go 10 rounds. Rocky fights the fight of his life that evening and gets beaten up terribly. His face is bloodied, with cuts over his eyes to a degree that they are swelling shut. Yet the highlight of the fight for Rocky and all that are watching is when the bell for the final round sounds. The champion gets up from his stool and stares across the ring at Rocky who, in spite of being all beaten up, is still there and ready to come out and face the last round. The champion shakes his head in disbelief, as if to say, "I can't believe this guy. He's beaten up, bloody and tired, and doesn't have a chance. Odds say he should quit, yet he still endures."

Rocky goes out and fights the last round. There is no 'quit' in him, no matter how tired, and beaten up he is. He endures beyond what everyone in the arena believes is possible. That is the sign of a true champion and fighter in life.

Sixth, rely on others to help and assist. Get some people in your corner that can help you deal with the fears and weaknesses that you are coping with. Rocky had a great personal trainer who helped him tremendously. His girlfriend (and soon to be wife) played such an important role in his life. He could not have done it on his own strength and skills.

Can you recall when Jesus went to pray in the garden of Gethsemane? This was a very difficult time in His life. After His journey there, He asked Peter, James and John to go with Him. When they arrived, he told them to keep watch and pray. In other words, "strengthen me with your presence." He asked them to pray and stay awake. He's telling them, "I need you in my corner."

There is nothing wrong with calling on others to help and assist. That great phrase I remind you of again is, "We're going to make it!" Who is in your corner? Do you need someone to keep watch and pray for you? Go ahead and ask whenever you feel fearful and weak.

Seventh, feed your mind. Strengthen your walk with the word of God. Let the word of God and the promises spoken in the Word saturate your mind and thought process. Let it speak to you and your circumstances. Speak the word of God to yourself. Hear the promises of God. Let the word of God feed your mind, your emotions and give you balance and strength against fears and weaknesses. Listed below are some great promises of encouragement and support from the word of God. Talk about who's got your back!

"Not only so, but we also glory in our sufferings, because we know that suffering produces perseverance; perseverance, character; and character, hope. And hope does not put us to shame, because God's love has been poured out into our hearts through the Holy Spirit, who has been given to us." (Romans 5:3-5)

"Come to Me, all who are weary and heavy-laden, and I will give you rest. Take my yoke upon you and learn from Me, for I am gentle and humble in heart and you shall find rest for your souls." (Matthew 11:28-29)

"These things I have spoken to you, that in Me you may have peace. In the world you have tribulation, but take courage; I have overcome the world." (John 16:33)

"Cast your burden upon the Lord and He will sustain you: He will never allow the righteous to be shaken." (Psalm 55:22)

"The Lord is my light and my salvation; Whom shall I fear? The Lord is the defense of my life; Whom shall I dread? When evildoers came upon me to devour my flesh, my adversaries and my enemies, they stumbled and fell. Though a host encamps against me, my heart will not fear. Though war arises against me, in spite of this I shall be confident." (Psalm 27:1-3)

"Peace I leave with you; My peace I give to you; not as the world gives, do I give to you. Let not your heart be troubled, nor let it be fearful." (John 14:27)

"For I am convinced that neither death, nor life, nor angels, nor principalities, nor things present, nor things to come, nor powers, nor height, nor depth, nor any other created thing, shall be able to separate us from the love of God, which is in Christ Jesus our Lord." (Romans 8:38-39)

"I sought the Lord and He answered me and delivered me from all my fears." (Psalm 34:4)

"I can do all through Christ who strengthens me." (Philippians 4:13)

"Be anxious for nothing, but in everything by prayer and supplication with thanksgiving let your requests be made known to God. And the peace of God, which surpasses all understanding, shall guard your hearts and your minds in Christ Jesus." (Philippians 4:6-7)

"Do not fear, for I am with you; Do not anxiously look about you, for I am your God. I will strengthen you, surely I will help you." (Isaiah 41:10)

"The Lord is my shepherd, I shall not want." (Psalm 23:1)

"Trust in the Lord with all of your heart and do not lean on your own understanding. In all your ways acknowledge Him and He will make your paths straight." (Proverbs 3:6-7)

"And we know that God causes all things to work together for good to those who love God, to those who are called according to His purpose." (Romans 8:28)

"God is our refuge and strength, a very present help in trouble. Therefore we will not fear, though the earth shall change, and though the mountains slip into the heart of the sea;" (Psalm 46:1-2)

LIST OF FEAR BUSTERS

To sum it up, here are the seven fear busters:

1. Admit your fears.

2. Face your fears.

3. Realize fear can help you.

4. Look fear in the eyes and show courage.

5. Endure and be a fighter.

6. Rely on others for assistance.

7. Feed your mind on the word and promises of God.

WHAT ABOUT YOU?

I'm sure that each one of us can relate in some way to what I've been talking about regarding fear and weakness. They do play a role in our lives at times. There are times of challenge out there. It doesn't matter if we are teenagers, young adults, middle-aged or old. It doesn't matter whether we are male or female or what the color of our skin is. And it surely doesn't matter if we are rich, or living from paycheck to paycheck. We are all the same. There are times in our lives when we are faced with things that will help us realize who we truly are, and makes us aware of how we are going to deal with it.

As you think about your life, can you recall your own little league stories? Maybe they took place in your adult years. Have there been fears and/or weaknesses that have dictated your life or decisions you have made? Is there a job that you didn't apply for because you didn't feel worthy or capable? Are there words that should have been spoken but weren't? What about right now? Are you dealing with something that is challenging you? Are any fears or any sense of weakness playing a part within you that is affecting your thinking and processing of a single situation, or as a father, son, employee, boss, or family member?

Do you ever get scared and wonder? Do you ever think over and over again about a situation that you are facing? Do you ever feel like you don't have the strength to continue? Has something been going on for a long time that is wearing you out? Do you ever wonder just how much more can you take?

WHAT ABOUT US?

1. Have you ever been afraid about situation, challenge or circumstance in your life? Take time and think back for a bit.

2. Can you share any of your personal stories of fears and weaknesses with the group?

3. Can you recall a time when fear got the best of you? How did it affect you, your decisions, and the outcome?

4. Think for a moment about the seven fear busters. Talk about them and share about any of them that apply to you and the challenges in your life.

    1) Admit your fears.

    2) Face your fears.

    3) Realize fear can help you.

    4) Look fear in the eyes and show courage.

    5) Endure and be a fighter.

    6) Rely on others for assistance.

    7) Feed your mind on the word and promises of God.

CHAPTER THREE

THE THREE T'S

Everyone who enters the armed forces is required to go through 12 weeks of basic training. Basic training is a person's introduction into the military; skills are taught and you begin your training as a soldier. From basic training, I went on to advanced infantry training that lasted 18 weeks. That was where I learned how to be a soldier, ready for combat and war. It was the combination of both of those experiences that prepared me for my mission, which was to be an infantry soldier in Vietnam.

I was taught much and learned even more during those 30 weeks of training. It was hard, endless and seemed, at times, like more than one could comprehend or go through. Along with all the training, much time was given to physical fitness; making our bodies stronger and getting in shape. The various forms of training worked together to make each one of us a true soldier, capable of facing and handling war.

I realized there was a thread that was woven throughout the entire training process that proved to be of tremendous value to my development as a soldier, as well as my safety and well being. It took nearly half of my basic training for it to sink in, but when it did, it put the whole purpose of the training into a crystal clear perspective.

This thread, I learned, was the value and the importance of the three T's. The three T's are **training, time,** and **trust.** The lessons and truths I learned concerning the three T's made a tremendous impact on me.

The things I learned during those seven months about training, time, and trust has remained with me throughout my lifetime and has helped me through many situations and challenges. I would like to share with you some of the lessons and truths I learned concerning the three T's. Be aware that the three T's are not just for soldiers but can be so applicable and valuable to each one of us.

TRAINING

Training was the key word for the mission. It seemed like all we did was train. Day in and day out, I trained to become and to achieve. There was a course of instruction that had to be learned. Day after day, week after week, we trained, we studied, we observed and we listened. Then we had to do it—we had to perform all that we had learned and trained for.

It wasn't like I had never heard this word before. I had trained and grown in past experiences of my life, from learning to ride a bike, to growing as an athlete, to some of my early job experiences. We can all relate to training as we grow up, yet this was different. This training was more than just learning.

It was during the weeks and months that followed that I learned the true definition and purpose of training. Training was listening, learning, observing, knowing, practicing and discipline. It was all these things working together for a purpose that would make me a better soldier, ready for the mission.

First of all, the real training was learning from others. Others who had first-hand knowledge and experience. Accessing the knowledge from people who wanted me to become better equipped, skilled and able to succeed. This training was essential. I needed to learn and apply these skills to my life. They had what I needed. I did not yet possess the knowledge and skills that were needed at this time in my life. I had to admit my shortcomings and I had to learn from others.

Sometimes, the things I learned were taught in a way that seemed harsh and like a very personal attack. I remember when we were learning about coming upon enemy fire when on patrol or on an ambush. When you hear gunfire, you are taught to hit the ground as low as possible. Lie as flat as possible. Taste the ground below you. Get so low you can lick the dirt. Then, close your eyes and see with your ears. Do not look around at first to see where the shots are coming from because that makes you more of a target and could endanger your life. Let your hearing be your eyes. Your hearing can point you in the direction of the incoming gunfire.

We learned these two simple principles that were proven to be valuable in keeping ourselves from getting shot. Some guys did not take this advice seriously. They did not get low enough to the ground. I remember a few times when the training sergeant came up to some of these soldiers and smacked them on the side of their helmets so hard it knocked their helmets to the ground. I can recall one guy looking up and yelling at the sergeant, "Hey, what's up? That really hurt my head!"

The sergeant responded, "You think me hitting you on the head hurt you today? Wait until a bullet hits you in the head or some other part of your body. Then you'll know what hurt really feels like. Now, get your head down and kiss that ground! That will keep you from getting hit by a bullet and my hand."

While this seemed like a harsh, personal attack, it truly was not. We were being trained to react in a way that would benefit each one of us and not the enemy. This training had to be learned and become second nature because it could easily mean the difference between life and death.

Secondly, training was listening and paying attention. Listening meant really hearing what was being said; taking it in fully and completely, and paying attention to those people who had the words and knowledge that would benefit me. I could not drift off into some other world. The sounds I was hearing had to enter through my eardrums and make its way into my brain. Listening became a skill I definitely had to improve on.

Thirdly, training meant knowledge gained by experience. Over and over I practiced what I was taught. I had to push myself beyond my comfort zone so many times. Phrases like, "I can't do that", or "This is not for me" could not be thought, spoken or accepted as an option.

Repetition became a way of learning until I proved myself worthy and capable. Over and over I repeated what I was learning. I practiced many times and often. Sometimes, at night before I would drift off to sleep, I would practice in my mind what I had learned. I was gaining knowledge by listening, learning and experiencing.

Finally, training taught me that I could not quit and I could not run away. I had to abandon any feeling that "This is not for me" or "I am incapable of achieving or learning." Running away was not an option. I had to learn, and *would* learn. Over the months that followed, I trained long and hard. I came to understand the value of training and learned how things fit together. I was living, breathing and truly understanding the meaning of training.

At this point, my entire life and its outcome depended so much on training. What I was learning and what I put into my training was critical. Discipline became a vital part of the training. I learned I could become more and be better equipped. Training was fundamental. I learned to embrace it, desire it, crave it, and ultimately realize that I desperately needed it.

TIME

Throughout my training, I learned the truth about the second "T" which is time. Time is the most important asset a person has. Each one of us has the advantage of time. We all are given an equal share. Not one person is given more than another. It doesn't matter how old you are, what race you are, or what gender you are. Each one of us is given the same amount of time... no matter where you are in line! By this I mean that each minute contains 60 seconds; each hour contains 60 minutes; and each day contains 24 hours, etc. No more and no less, all the same for each of us.

Time is, and has always been, a part of my life, from getting up in the morning to going to sleep at night. Time is spent going to school and being in class, playing after school, working, doing chores, and doing homework. Time is also set aside to go to church, to eat, and time to call it a day.

My time spent is similar to yours and so many others. Time dominates everything and everyone. How many clocks do you have in your house? Do you wear a watch? Does your cell phone display the time? What time is it right now? How much time do you have to read this book before you have to do something else? You get the picture. But it was in the military that I truly learned the value, importance and discipline of time.

THE VALUE OF TIME

Time is so incredibly valuable. It's a person's most significant asset. Let me repeat that. *Time is our most significant asset!* No one has more than you or less than you and we all value time immensely.

Let's think about time for a moment. Time is the seconds, minutes, hours and days that make up our weeks, months and years. It's the same time that we are all experiencing at this very moment. We are all expending time at the same pace; my hour contains the same amount of time as your hour.

When one talks about time, we are generally talking about life itself. Time is life. Ben Franklin was quoted as saying, "Do not squander time, because that is the stuff life is made of." That stuff and all of our existence is tied into time.

Time is valuable because it goes by so quickly. It really feels like the older we get, the faster time goes by. You've heard it before, "how time flies." This is so true. Think about yourself for a moment. How old are you? How many years since you graduated from high school? Are you as young as you used to be? How long have you been married? What are the ages of your children...or grandchildren? Didn't we just experience Christmas or summer? Wasn't the Y2K scare just last year?

Time is so valuable because it is so brief. It truly doesn't last forever. If you really want to understand how brief time is, go visit a cemetery. Take a look at any grave marker. Beneath each name will be two dates...an entry date and an exit date. For example:

John Jones
1948 – 2005

Time (or life) is summarized in that brief little dash. The little dash between our entry date and our exit date. It is that little dash (and none of us knows how much time is represented and encapsulated in that meaningful dash) that will one day appear under our own name. No one ever has enough time. Yet, we are all allocated the same amount, 168 hours each week. No one is given one hour more or less. Yet some can do so much more with that same amount of time.

Time can also be very stubborn and uncooperative. Have you ever noticed that? When you want time to zip by, it can just drag on. When you want it to go slowly, it speeds by so fast. Have you ever noticed that two weeks on a vacation is never the same as two weeks on a diet? Two weeks in Hawaii is never the same as two weeks on the job. An hour at the dentist just isn't the same as an hour at the park. You get the picture.

So, the time we are given is to be used. We all use time in various ways. We can be creative with it and use it wisely, or throw it away like a fool. We can waste it or have it serve a purpose for us. We all exchange time for something, whether it's work, play, sleep, rest or just watching television. We all exchange our time for something in return. You're doing it right now. You are exchanging some of your time to read this book. It was your choice to read this book when you could have been doing something else. You made the decision.

TIME IN MILITARY SERVICE

My two years of military service taught me much about time. There I learned the value, substance, and importance of time.

I can remember so clearly my first encounter with time in the military. It was my first day in the army. We had just finished breakfast and were driven to a supply depot where we were issued our military clothing. After going through the receiving process for nearly two hours, we had to pack all of our clothing into duffle bags. Then we were loaded into vehicles that were called "cattle trucks". The cattle trucks proceeded to take us to our barracks, which would be our home for the next 12 weeks of training.

When we arrived, a Drill Sergeant approached our truck. He went to the back of the truck, opened the tailgate and shouted, "Welcome to your home for the next 12 weeks. You have exactly one minute to get out of that truck and stand in formation. I have just used up 15 seconds of your time. That leaves you less than one minute. Lets go!"

You never saw a group of men move so quickly. Duffle bags were hurriedly thrown over the sides of the truck in every direction. Just for the record, you can unload a truck of 100 men in less than one minute. It truly can be done! I was there, and I was one of the fast-moving men.

This is where I became truly cognizant of the concept and meaning of time. I will never forget that day. Everything that happened in the next few weeks was centered on time. It was during these weeks of training that I truly learned about the second of the three T's.

WHAT I LEARNED ABOUT TIME

Time dominated every aspect of our training and existence. We were given just 12 weeks to train. There was so much to learn in this very short time! Each day was extremely important and jobs and responsibilities had to be learned. There was no "getting around to it" or putting it off. We had to stay on course because time mattered so much. Our training each day had to be accomplished.

We had to get up early. There was a time to rise and a time for lights out. Every day was the same. You couldn't choose when you wanted to get up. Every hour was structured and filled with classes and learning. There was a schedule that must be adhered to. Time dominated everything we did.

We had to be disciplined in our use of time. Discipline and time worked together as partners. There was a purpose behind both. There would be no "ifs, ands, or buts" about time. Time to wake up was at 5:00 a.m. and there was no sleeping in. You *will* get up, shower, shave and eat breakfast. You will be in formation by 7:30 a.m. The duties and the training will begin on time.

If the first training class began at 8:00 a.m., that meant *8:00 a.m.* If the next class was at 10:00 a.m., that meant 10:00 a.m., *not* 10:01 or any other time. We had to be disciplined with our time management. We could not fight it or complain about it and we had to follow orders.

We also learned to cherish time. Time was serving a purpose, from getting up in the morning to going to bed at night. We had to wake up early because there was so much that had to be done and accomplished each day. There were hours given for training when nothing else mattered. Time was given to take a break and rest. For those who smoked cigarettes, you could use this time to light up.

There was time each evening to get ready for the next day. Time to write a letter to the girl back home, family or loved ones. Time to stand in line for an hour to make a 5-minute phone call home. Time to go to bed and peacefully experience those remaining hours of the day...the wonderful purpose of rest ... to regain strength for your body, and hopefully sweet dreams.

Time was benefiting all of us in the barracks. It truly was the most valuable asset we were given. As I lived out each moment of time, I became better equipped for the tasks in front of me. The time encapsulated in those days and weeks were truly benefiting me. I was using time to the fullest and it was paying off.

TRUST

The "T" that proved the most vital and fundamental to me was *trust*. Trust was one of the most powerful words that affected my life over the next two years. It was a word I had heard many times before. That word was even printed on the back of the currency that I carried in my wallet.

It was in the service that I truly learned the *concept* of trust. I learned what it meant for someone to say they *trusted* someone, and to know that *they* could be trusted. It no longer was a word spoken, but a foundation for living and dealing with life.

THINKING ABOUT TRUST

Trust is the single most important factor in any relationship. If trust is absent or questionable, no matter what type of relationship (spouse, friend, employee, etc.), then that relationship is fundamentally weak. There is no way any relationship can be strong if the trust factor is missing. Have you ever heard it said about political candidates, "You can't trust them or the promises they make?" Sadly, this is often said of issues within a marriage, "I can't trust my husband (or wife)." Trust is truly the single most important factor in *any* relationship.

Let me give you a definition of trust. Trust is *complete* **confidence**, **reliance** and **hope** in the **ability** and **integrity** of a person.

To trust means to have complete and total confidence. That means 100%. Doubt doesn't even enter the thought process. One can rely on that person. Their word and being brings confidence. Hope is in the relationship because you believe in their ability. What they say and offer can come true. Their integrity as a person and their words and abilities are sure-footed and solid. There is no doubt in your mind of your trust in that person. That makes the relationship strong for all.

It was in the service that I learned and experienced the true meaning of trust. I had to trust the people who were training me. Their knowledge and words spoke truth for survival. I had no option but to have confidence and hope in their ability and integrity. To have any doubt could prove detrimental to my safety, and could ultimately cost me my life.

I had to have trust in the training, the expected outcome, and how it would all eventually piece together. It was like a puzzle with a 1000 pieces. It could be put together to create a picture and though it might be a bit difficult, it could be achieved.

I had to trust in a group of men who were being formed into a unit of brotherhood. I had to trust that we would have each other's back. I had to trust in others (the Air Force, medics, artillery and other support units) that would come into play during the war. We would function and succeed as a whole, but not as individuals.

Never in my life had the word 'trust' become so meaningful and alive within me. It meant hope and confidence as I faced the many challenges before me, and would become part of me within the next six months.

IN GOD WE TRUST

On the back of our currency is a phrase, "In God We Trust." The currency could be a $1 bill or a $100 bill. On each bill the same phrase is written. Have you ever wondered why that phase was put on our currency?

A few years back, I had the opportunity to speak at the baccalaureate service for a high school in southern California. My message was entitled "It is a matter of trust." As I began my talk, I stepped down from the stage onto the floor of the auditorium to where the 400 graduating seniors were seated.

Then, I pulled a $5 bill, a $20 bill and a $100 bill out of my wallet. I asked the young people if they could choose only one, which one would they choose? The choice by most was, of course, the $100 bill. (By the way, two young men did take me seriously. They left their seats and came up to me to receive the bill they chose. I laughed with them and told them that this was only an illustration. I was not rich enough to give away a $100 bill.)

I asked them why one was of more value to them. Of course their answer was the number written on the bill. A $20 bill is of more value than a $5 bill. The answer seemed very obvious to them.

I then proceeded to show them and explain to them why the true value is not in the number on the bill, but what is imprinted on the backside of the bill. I turned the $100 bill over and showed them the powerful phrase "In God We Trust"." That phrase was on every bill that I showed them. Belief in this phrase is where the true value for them and their lives exists.

The future of each one of these young people was ahead of them. This includes college, trade schools, careers, and employment. It means going forward to achieve success and purpose. It all stood before them in the months and years ahead. Achieving their full potential had little to do with money. However, it had a lot to do with the statement that appeared on each bill. To truly believe and live out a life of trusting in God would prove to be of the greatest value.

What about you right now? Where do you place your faith, confidence and hope? Who do you trust enough to place your hopes and your life in their hands? It's easy to say we trust in God. Yet will our lives, thoughts, and decisions exemplify us as a person who trusts in God? Therein lies the value of a person and how trust will affect the rest of their life.

Proverbs 3:5-6 says, "Trust in the LORD with all your heart and lean not on your own understanding; in all your ways acknowledge Him, and He will make your paths straight."

WHAT ABOUT US?

Let's talk about the three T's.

1. Where have you seen the value of training?

   Even now, are you called to train even harder for a task or challenge that you are facing?

2. What comes to your mind when you think of time in your life?

   Re-evaluate your weekly schedule. Where are you investing your time?

When it comes to your family, where do you spend your time? How much time is given to your wife? Your children? What makes up the content of the time given to your family?

List two or three things that you may want to do to restructure the "time commitments" in your life."

3. Who comes to your mind as being trustworthy? What makes you think of them as a person who can be trusted?

How trustworthy of a person are you?

When it comes to your word, how good is your word?

4. Do you trust in God? As you think of your answer, what evidence would come forth that proves your trust in God? Could it be said of you, "In God I trust?"

CHAPTER FOUR

FRIENDS OF ENCOURAGEMENT

Years ago I wrote a book entitled *Becoming a Stretcher Bearer*. It was a book about bringing healing and hope to a hurting world. All of us need encouragement and support. People who hurt are the people on stretchers. Each one of us, at some time in our life, has dealt with hurt, challenges and disappointments. It could be financial issues, shattered dreams, family issues, illness, self-worth issues, or a variety of disappointments.

To hurt is bad enough, but to hurt alone destroys people physically, mentally and spiritually. This truth has led me to engage in the practical ministry of Stretcher-Bearing...a ministry of encouragement and support. In this chapter, I will share some truths about being a stretcher-bearer. The truth behind being a stretcher-bearer goes right alongside the question, "Who's got your back?" It shouts out with encouragement that, "We're going to make it." It's a concept and teaching that I pray will be lived out among you and your group. The following is the story of the stretcher-bearers, as found in Mark 2:

> "A few days later, when Jesus again entered Capernaum, the people heard that he had come home. So many gathered that there was no room left, not even outside the door, and he preached the word to them. Some men came, bringing to him a paralytic, carried by four of them. Since they could not get him to Jesus because of the crowd, they made an opening in the roof above Jesus and, after digging through it, lowered the mat the paralyzed man was lying on. When Jesus saw their faith, he said to the paralytic, "Son, your sins are forgiven."

Now some teachers of the law were sitting there, thinking to themselves, "Why does this fellow talk like that? He's blaspheming! Who can forgive sins but God alone?"

Immediately Jesus knew in his spirit that this was what they were thinking in their hearts, and he said to them, "Why are you thinking these things? Which is easier: to say to the paralytic, 'Your sins are forgiven,' or to say, 'Get up, take your mat and walk'? But that you may know that the Son of Man has authority on earth to forgive sins . . . ." He said to the paralytic, "I tell you, get up, take your mat and go home." He got up, took his mat and walked out in full view of them all. This amazed everyone and they praised God, saying, "We have never seen anything like this!" (Mark 2:1-12)

FRIENDS OF ENCOURAGEMENT

Mark 2 is the account of a paralyzed man fortunate enough to have four loving and compassionate friends, who were also men of great faith. They acted on their faith and carried their paralyzed friend to Jesus. *"When Jesus saw their faith"*—the faith of the four stretcher-bearers—He acted on their faith and healed their crippled friend on the spot.

Acting on our faith with love and compassion for others—ministering to others with the gift of encouragement and support—is the ministry of stretcher-bearing. It is also believing that a true friend is someone who is always there when it matters, when it counts, and when it hurts.

The stretcher-bearer concept has been a vital part of my life and my desire is to teach others how to become stretcher-bearers themselves. As a pastor, I am called upon to listen, counsel and advise. My ministry to people in various situations has enabled me to understand the reasons behind that which destroys so many people. Individuals have actually come into my office and told me such things as, "No one cares about me. No one cares if I live or die. I have no one to turn to. I feel helpless and alone."

In Mark 2:1-12, as in any other story or parable in the Bible, the important point is not that a healing or miracle took place. It's what the Bible is trying to teach us *concerning* that miracle or parable.

You see, I believe each miracle in the Bible is recorded to teach us about various concepts of the Christian faith. If we understand the concept behind the teaching of the miracle—and sometimes it has to do with healing—then the miracle or the concept can take place in our lives today.

So, what then is the basis of the story in Mark 2:1-12 where the four men carry their friend on the stretcher? It's that the paralytic man truly needed his wonderfully determined friends to carry him and his problem to the feet of Jesus. He obviously couldn't have done it on his own.

The healing that took place in this account occurred, not primarily because of the man on the stretcher, or because Jesus had the gift to heal. The healing took place because of the faith, encouragement and support of the man's four devoted friends. They were determined to carry his stretcher. They were determined to find answers to each problem as it arose; finding the home, knowing where and how to cut the hole in the roof and then lowering their friend at the feet of Jesus. Jesus vividly saw their faith and He used their faith to give healing to the man on the stretcher.

Sometimes situations make stretcher-bearing seem hopeless. That is why stretcher-bearers need that imaginative faith that turns problems into challenges because the welfare of a friend is involved. A stretcher-bearer is that *"friend who sticks closer than a brother"* (Proverbs 18:24). That person of encouragement and support who stands by the side of a friend no matter what the difficulty.

Mark 2:1-12 gives the biblical understanding of the stretcher-bearer concept. It makes use of a very visual metaphor—a stretcher. Here were four friends, caring for someone who was on a stretcher. This particular story deals with physical illness, yet people can be on a stretcher for a number of reasons; physical illness, social, spiritual or even emotional illness. We need to be prepared for that time when God may call us to lift someone's stretcher.

A BIBLICAL UNDERSTANDING OF SUPPORT

Throughout scripture, many examples of how people encouraged one another are revealed. There are examples of stretcher-bearers in both the Old and New Testaments. In 1 Samuel 18, we read the story of Jonathan and David. We learn of their special friendship and of the way they encouraged and supported each another. In Exodus 17, we read of Aaron and Hur and how they held up the arms of Moses in the defeat of the Amalakites. These two men allowed themselves to be used to support Moses at a very critical time in his life.

In the New Testament, Paul encouraged a young minister named Timothy. Where would Timothy have been without the encouragement and support he received through the letters Paul wrote to him? Galatians 6:2 says, *"Bear one another's burdens and so fulfill the law of Christ."* Also, found in 1 Peter 5:13, is evidence of the support and encouragement Peter gave to the young disciple, Mark.

But what about Jesus? Was the gift of encouragement and support vital for Him? Was it vital for His ministry and for His well being? We read that when Jesus went to the Garden of Gethsemane, He did not want to go alone. He truly wanted to be supported by three special friends, Peter, James and John (see Mark 14:33). This is a classic example of our Lord desiring support and encouragement in His own life.

The Lord's disciple, John, was a special friend and encourager to Jesus. He was a beloved disciple who played a vital part in the support of Jesus (John 13:33; 20:21). This was especially evident when Jesus, through His suffering on the cross, encouraged John to take care of His mother, Mary. John responded to Jesus as that special friend by caring for Mary as he would his own mother (John 19:25-27). He became a stretcher-bearer, a person of encouragement and support.

A SPECIAL FRIEND

As you can see, the teaching of encouragement and support is found throughout scripture. A classic example is described in Proverbs 18:24: *"A man of many companions may come to ruin, but there is a friend who sticks closer than a brother."* The Living Bible puts it this way: *"There are friends who pretend to be a friend, but there is a friend who sticks closer than a brother."*

I have two questions to pose to you for your personal consideration and growth. First, if you had your Bible in front of you and you underlined Proverbs 18:24, whose name would you write in your Bible as your special friend? Take a moment to think about this right now. This question is so very important.

Secondly, do you think anyone would write your name in his or her Bible? Yes or no? Answer this question as honestly as you can.

Now spend some time thinking deeply about both of these questions.

Do we have that special friend, or are we that special friend to someone else? Are we really brothers and sisters to one another? You see, Christianity is more than just going to church. Christianity is that intimate relationship with God, lived out among one another. It is people encouraging and supporting each another in the name of Jesus Christ. Remember, going to church doesn't make you a Christian any more than standing in a garage makes you a car.

PERSONAL STRETCHER BEARERS

The basic principle of the entire concept of stretcher-bearing is a simple one and is revealed by the answer to the question, "What caused the miracle in the stretcher- bearer story of Mark 2?" We find the answer in verse 5, which is simply, *"When Jesus saw their faith."*

Whose faith? The words "their faith" refer to the faith of the four men who carried the stretcher. Jesus was moved when He saw the faith of these men. Yes, Jesus did the healing, but the miracle occurred because the men brought their friend into the presence of Jesus. They had faith and acted on it. Without their caring and support, the miracle might not have taken place.

THE STRETCHER WAITS

Another thought I want to share is that the stretcher is for each one of us. Each one of us will, at some time, be the man or woman on the stretcher. Now that might not be the best news you hear today, but friend, it's going to happen eventually. It could be something that will affect you physically, mentally, socially or spiritually.

Someone in your family may be hurting in some way. This would then cause you to feel hurt, too. All of us have experienced the illness or death of someone dear to us; a husband or wife, a parent, a grandparent, an aunt or uncle, a co-worker or a friend. Any event can put us on a stretcher and we will definitely feel the need of supportive people around us. There will be moments in our lives when each one of us is that person on the stretcher.

WHAT DESTROYS PEOPLE

Each one of us, at any moment in life, can suddenly be placed on a stretcher, unable to deal effectively with a problem or challenge by ourselves. We are all going to experience good times and bad times. People are not necessarily destroyed or disheartened just because they find themselves on a stretcher. What can destroy people is when they find themselves on a stretcher and they feel no one cares. A person can become so shattered that he or she gives up on faith, gives up on hope, gives up on God, and can give up on life.

Let me share with you the words of an actual suicide note. I only share this to stress how important it is to show others that we care about their problems.

"Life is not worth living. No once cares for me. Right now I would be better off with the Lord. No one will care if I live or die. I doubt anyone would miss me. Because of this, I choose to die."

What seemed to destroy this man was not only being on a stretcher, but also feeling that no one could or would carry his stretcher and help him through his troubled time. He felt alone and uncared for by anyone.

I am firmly convinced that when you have no one to carry your stretcher, you are on dangerous ground. We all need to learn how to reach out and become stretcher-bearers to others. We must allow God to use us to encourage others when they are dealing with stretcher experiences. To be a stretcher-bearer, using the gift of encouragement and support in another's life, is a powerful, personal ministry blessed by our Lord.

LET'S THINK

Below is a picture of a stretcher. Write your name in the middle of the stretcher. Now think, are there four people who would carry you if you were physically, spiritually, socially or emotionally on a stretcher? Can you think of four people who would lift your stretcher? If so, fill in their names. If you do not have four, what about three? Or two? Or even one?

1. _____   2. _____

3. _____   4. _____

If you are able to identify some stretcher-bearers, I encourage you now to get in touch with these people. Follow through today and let them know by letter, e-mail, telephone, or in person that you believe in them as stretcher-bearers for you. Let them know what it means to be encouraged and supported by people like them. Tell them about what you have been reading here. Tell them as you read it, you were asked to think of someone who would carry your stretcher, and when you did, you thought of them.

Can you imagine the bond that could be developed by sharing this? Imagine how they are going to feel after hearing these words from you. When you reach out and tell someone that you realize how much they truly care for you, relationships are strengthened.

If you have only one person's name on your list, or if you have none, don't feel bad. Perhaps this is a concept of the Christian faith that God, through is Holy Spirit, is trying to teach you. As you continue to read about and understand the stretcher-bearer theme, God will bring those special people into your life. You, in turn, can become a stretcher-bearer to someone else.

CLOSING THOUGHTS

I am convinced that being on a stretcher is not what destroys people. It's being on the stretcher and believing that no one cares that does.

WHAT ABOUT US?

1. Do you have a special friend as talked about in Proverbs 18:24? If so, who would it be? If you don't have that special friend, why not?

2. Do you think anyone would write your name as his or her special friend?

3. What have you contributed to friendships that are a meaningful part of your life?

4. What contributions have your friends made to the relationships?

5. I encourage you to make contact with the friends that came to mind and let them know what they mean to you.

CHAPTER FIVE

IT'S A MATTER OF TRUST

"Trust is the single most important factor in any relationship."

In the past two decades, I have become aware of something that continues to affect our nation, society, and families in a most hurtful and degenerating manner. We are becoming a society of people who lack trust. The concept of trust within our society is becoming less and less vital and honored among people in different walks of life.

Now I know this opening paragraph sounds pretty straightforward and critical. Yet as I look around and watch what is happening now, I see something that has been building over the years. I see a "cancer" attacking our world and growing at such a rate that is destroying our families and our society. It appears to be in the process of destroying our nation as well. It all centers on the word "TRUST." Because of the critical significance of trust, it is also discussed in some detail in Chapter 3 as of the three T's.

I think we need to examine this word and take an honest inventory of our lives, including our spirituals lives, and determine exactly how trust factors into them. I believe this self-examination will prove of vital importance when it comes to who's *really* got your back.

It's been said that trust is the single most important factor in any relationship. If trust is questioned in a relationship, that relationship will be weak. You can't have a strong relationship when trust is questioned, no matter what the reason. It is a foundational element when you think of who's got your back. One can't honestly allow someone to "have their back" if the element of trust is missing or weakened.

A WORKING DEFINITION OF TRUST

1. Trust means to have *complete* **confidence**, **reliance** and **hope** in the **ability** and **integrity** of someone.

2. Trust means to have *unquestionable* **belief** and **reliance** upon someone.

Those two descriptions sum up a true understanding of how trust works between people. When one says they trust someone, it means they have a confidence in that person that is certain. They know the integrity of that person and believe and hope in them.

This belief and hope is solid. It is unquestionable. Doubt doesn't play a part in that relationship. There is a solid belief and reliance on the person, their words, and their actions. This trust is good today, tomorrow, next week, and next year. It is lived out and accepted with complete confidence.

QUESTIONS FOR THOUGHT

Think for a moment about your world and your definition of trust. First of all, whom would you consider people or groups of people that you have little trust in, or have lost trust in over the years? Some of these people you may know personally, and others you may have read about or heard about on the news. Either way, you have doubts or less trust in them. Give yourself a moment here to think.

Secondly, whom would you consider people or groups of people that you trust in, or have learned to trust over the years? Again, some of these people you may know personally, and others you may have read about or heard about on the news. Are people coming to mind that you can say, "I have trust in them?" Give yourself another moment to think.

Now with that is mind, why did you select the people you feel are not trustworthy? Was it something they said or did, maybe something you heard from someone else? In contrast, what about those you consider trustworthy. Why did you reach that conclusion about them?

Here's another question for you. Was it easier to come up with examples of people who were trustworthy or not trustworthy? Did you have more examples in one of the categories than the other? This is just something to think about as we look into the importance of trust between people.

Over the years, I have asked this question to many people. Surprisingly, more people find it easier to name people they did not trust, over people they had complete trust in. I believe all of this is saying something to us—something that needs to be addressed.

TAKE A LOOK AROUND

From my perspective, I look at our society and see an abundance of distrust between people. Especially when it comes to politics. How many politicians have been caught telling lies or doing dishonest things? I can't tell you how many times I've heard the statement, "You can't trust a politician." So many people are turned off to and disappointed in our government because of lack of trust in their word, their promises, and their actions. What some politicians promise on the campaign trail is far different than what they do when they are elected to office.

Take a look into the world of sports. Over the years, there has been an investigation into the use of steroids as performance enhancing drugs. The power, strength and body makeup of so many athletes has changed. The investigation into the use of steroids has made it all the way to the halls of our government. Athletes have testified under oath that they are not using steroids, yet, their testimony is being proven as not true. Others are confessing to selling, administering, and procuring drugs for the athletes. Many find it very easy to lie under oath.

Look at marriages and families in our society today. The number of marriages where vows are being broken and infidelity and betrayals are taking place is staggering. The percentage is very high and not getting any better. Trust is breaking down not only in marriages but also between parents and children. So many parents are finding themselves unable to trust their children. Society is affecting so many of our children, causing them to lie to parents when it comes to basic values, ethics and morality. In contrast, we also have parents lying to their children about those same (lack of) values, ethics and morals.

We can even take a look at ministers, priests and pastors in various churches of God. There are so many examples of leaders who have broken trust because of immoral actions and regretful decisions they have made. The Catholic Church, for instance, has admitted to sex scandals between priests and children over the decades. It's been front-page news across our nation. It's bad enough that the situations have occurred, but the cover up of so many of the incidents can really affect the trust that one has in that specific organization. Sadly, these same events and cover-ups have occurred within the Boy Scouts of America.

I was at a conference when one of these ministerial incidents was making the news. I had just finished speaking at one of the sessions and was on my way to the break-time venue for some coffee and Danish. As I was putting some cream in my coffee, I couldn't help overhearing a conversation that was taking place behind me among a group of ladies.

They were discussing an incident involving a minister who had been caught having an affair. It was all over the news. As they continued to discuss the incident, one of the ladies remarked, "When it comes to ministers, I believe you can't trust any of them. They all have issues of distrust. We are just not aware of them."

Now I have to be honest with you. That statement really got my attention. I walked over to them, introduced myself, and confessed that I had overheard part of their conversation. I began to tell them I was really shaken by the statement I heard about the lack of trust the one lady had for all ministers because of the action of the one minister in the news.

I then asked them if I could share my thoughts on parts of their conversation and conclusions, and they allowed me to do so. I told them that I agree that there are probably some ministers who have proven to no longer be trustworthy. I clarified that I don't know all the ministers across this nation, but I do believe her statement to be unfounded. I explained that I could make that statement with conviction because I am a minister, and I believe that as a minister I have earned trust and confidence. I can only speak for myself, but that truth alone proves her way of thinking as false.

Because of bad examples everywhere, there is much distrust between people. It's getting out of hand. It's affecting a huge number of people and their relationships with very negative and damaging results. Each one of us needs to place a high value on trust. It's a vital element towards strong and healthy relationships, marriages, families, and a strong and healthy nation. I have to ask myself, am I trustworthy? In the roles I play in life, am I a person to be trusted? That afternoon with those ladies, I felt I needed to respond. I needed to defend the multitude of trustworthy and faithful pastors, priests, and ministers, and reinforce the value of trust. I could, however, agree with them in principle, that when trust is broken, it does affect people and relationships in a negative way. We all need to be people who are worthy of trust.

Now as we continue to think about "Who's got your back", do you see how important trust is in answering that question? As you think about yourself and times in life that are challenging, who are the people you know that would, without a doubt, *really* have your back? Who have proven trustworthy?

IN GOD WE TRUST

I want to talk about a topic that, at times in our spiritual life, we need to take a close and honest inventory of. I want to talk about trusting God. I want to bring to the forefront some truths about having trust in God. Trust is vital in knowing God and His will for our life. To have trust in God that is confident, hopeful and with unquestionable belief is the kind of trust that says, without a doubt, "God has my back!"

QUESTIONS OF TRUST—SOMETHING TO THINK ABOUT

Do you trust God? Where do you place your faith, confidence and hope? Do you trust that God has a great plan for your life? Do you trust in God that He will never leave you? Do you trust in God that He is the shepherd and you are His sheep? Do you trust and believe God is part of your life and is concerned for you? Do you trust that God has your back?

It's easy to say, "I trust God" because I'm a believer. Yet, do our emotions and thoughts agree with that statement? Sometimes trust is not always an easy part of our Christian walk and proves very difficult to live out. We say words of trust and want to believe them, yet sometimes life has a way of making us doubt the trustworthiness of God. Trust is easier said than done.

Proverbs 3:1-6 reads: *"My son, do not forget my teaching, but keep my commands in your heart for they will prolong your life many years and bring you peace and prosperity. Let love and faithfulness never leave you; bind them around your neck, write them on the tablet of your heart. Then you will win favor and a good name in the sight of God and man. Trust in the Lord will all your heart and lean not on your own understanding; in all your ways acknowledge Him, and He will make your paths straight."*

Psalm 139:23-24 reads: *"Search me, God, and know my heart; test me and know my anxious thoughts. See if there is any offensive way in me, and lead me in the way everlasting."*

Proverbs 16:3 reads: *"Commit to the Lord whatever you do and your plans will succeed."*

SOME TRUST STATEMENTS ABOUT GOD

I want to share some trust statements about God that have given me encouragement and strength throughout my life. They are described below. Over the years, these statements of trust have grown within me and have proven their value and worth in my life time after time, especially during the challenging times that I have faced.

I am often reminded of these trust statements and question if I truly believe them and have complete trust in them. Over the years, times of challenges and hardship have attacked these trust statements and have caused me to question their truth and validity.

Through all these difficult times and challenges, I continue to be drawn to these trust statements and can now say with confidence that I believe they are true and they give me hope and assurance. I pray you will understand the truths of these trust statements, and that they will impact your life as they have impacted mine. These statements about trust in God aren't just for me—they're for you, too. Hear them out and let the truth of these statements bring you complete confidence, reliance and hope in the ability and integrity of God. He does have your back!

GOD IS TRUSTWORTHY

God is trustworthy and is worthy of our complete confidence. You can depend on Him. You can have unquestionable belief and reliance upon. His word is valid and truthful. God is not a liar.

We can question and doubt other people, what they tell us, and the promises they make. We can even question God. But that doesn't diminish the fact that God is to be trusted.

Most of us know the story of Job and the trials and tribulations in his life that he had to face. There were times where his friends told Job to question God. There were moments where he sat alone, wondering and questioning God. Even though Job questioned, doubted and wondered, it didn't weaken the fact that God is trustworthy. God is not to blame; He is not the enemy. And most of all, He is on our side.

Imprinted on our currency and coins are four words that are truly worth more than the value of the bill or coin itself—**In God We Trust**. Those four words speak volumes for us as individuals and as nation. They remind us of a relationship between God and His people. They remind us that our nation was built on the principle of God. They remind us of the truth and value of our love and loyalty for God and His love and loyalty for us.

There have been rumors about removing the words "In God We Trust" from our currency and coins. Those who seek removal of those words want to see our nation continually drawn away from God. They want to lead our nation down a path that will lead to ruin and inner destruction. They want to keep from us the truth that God is to be trusted and that each one of us can have complete reliance and hope in God.

GOD LOVES YOU

That's right! God loves you. Three truthful and simple words. Words validated in John 3:16 which reads, *"For God so loved the world, that He gave His only begotten Son, that whoever believes in Him will not perish, but will have eternal life."* The fact is, God loves this world. He loves every nation and every person. He loves you!

There is a short song written years ago, sung primarily by children entitled, "Jesus Loves Me." I'm sure you remember it. I'll bet some of you can sing it, or at least hum it right now. Go ahead, I dare you!

> Jesus loves me this I know.
> For the Bible tell me so.
> Little ones to him belong.
> They are weak, but He is strong.
>
> Yes, Jesus loves me.
> Yes, Jesus loves me.
> Yes, Jesus loves me.
> The Bible tells me so.

Guys, I have to be honest with you. We all need to be singing this song and believing the words. This is not just a song for *young* children. After all, we are *all* children of God. This song was intended for all of us. The trustworthy announcement repeated a number of times in the song, "Jesus loves me." A song about the unquestionable belief and reliance upon the love of God for you and me. I encourage you right now to hum this chorus or even sing it out loud. Don't be embarrassed. The truth of the song needs to speak to us. Go ahead, hum it. I'll do the same.

GOD CARES ABOUT ME

Not only does God love you, He also cares about you. To care about someone means to be aware and to become involved. To care is an expression of love, involvement and relationship with someone. When you care, you are not just on the sidelines watching. You are involved and trying to help.

God is aware and cares about you. He will and does get involved in our lives. Many times we are not even aware of His involvement, concern or caring for us. Remember the poem, "Footprints In The Sand"? That is what I'm talking about. We never walk alone. God knows, sees and cares. We may not even be aware of it at times.

There is one particular Psalm that God has used to speak to me during some of my darkest and most challenging times in my life. It speaks of a longing and desperate need for God during those difficult times of life's struggles. It ends with a reminder that God is there and cares. I'm talking about Psalm 42. Hear the words of this Psalm. For those of you who can relate to the words, I pray they are used to encourage you and offer you hope in your life challenges.

Psalm 42—A Song in the Night

As a desert wanderer longs for springs of cool water,
so my thirsty soul reaches out for you, O God.
How I long for a deeper sense of Your presence,
For a faith that will embrace You
without fear or doubt!
Yet while I weep in longing, people about me say,
"If God is not dead, where is He?"

I remember so well the faith of my childhood.
How real God was to me in those days

when I prayed and sang praises
and I listened to His Word
in the fellowship of family and friends!
Then why am I so depressed now?
Why cannot I recapture the joy and confidence
of those years?
I remember the stories of Your love
that I had been taught;
how merciful and all-powerful were Your dealings
with Your children throughout history!
Yet now my heart is empty,
and waves of doubt flood over my soul.

I pray, but the heavens, too, are empty.
It is almost as if God had forgotten all about me.
And while I struggle with the sickness of doubt,
People about me say,
"If God is not dead, where is He?"

O foolish heart, why do you seethe in unrest?
God has not changed;
His love for me is ever the same.
I must renew my faith is God;
I must again shout His praises
even when I do not feel His presence.
For truly He is God,
and He is my help and my hope.

Here is a person longing for and needing God. Sometimes life situations cause us to feel that God is far away. This Psalm is a song of hope for each one of us during our night times. By day the Lord directs His love, and at night His song can be within us.

May this Psalm affirm that we belong to God and have assurance of that truth. May it help set us free from the darkness. May it help to sustain us in our days and nights of our journey. May it help us to let go of the sickness of doubt.

When the road we walk becomes steeper, when the night we endure grows darker, when the load we carry becomes heavier, and when the pain we feel reaches despair, God has a song in the night for us.

It may come as a lyric set to music (Jesus Loves Me). It could be a precious promise from His Word. It could be the comfort from a friend. It could be the wings of an insight that helps get us through a particular situation. It can be a remembrance from the past.

But in many ways, God comes to His children in their night seasons with His presence and His promises. God has a song in the night. Let us renew our faith in God, shout His praises, even if we don't feel like it. He is God, and He is our help and our hope.

A PERSONAL CONFESSION

I would like to make a personal confession. "God loves me" and "God cares about me" were the hardest of the trust statements for me to accept and truly believe in. To believe that God loves me (Mike Slater) and that God really cares about my insignificant life were hard to swallow. I'm sorry, but for many years I just could not accept or agree with those statements.

There were so many other people who were more important and more deserving of God's love and personal care. Come on, how much can a young man from southern California really matter to God? For years, if you had asked me to name people that God really loved and cared for, I wouldn't have been one of them. I felt insignificant and unworthy of His personal love and care.

Over the years, my thinking has changed. I truly believe in these two trust statements. God does love Mike Slater. Yes, me, Mike Slater. God does care for me, Mike Slater. He loves and cares for me and I am of value and importance to Him. He is aware of my life, and is caring and involved in it. I can and will sing the song, "Jesus Loves Me." I will continue to sing and believe in that truth for as long as I live.

GOD'S CARE IS CONSTANT

Another trust statement is that God's care is constant. He not only cares for us, but His care is constant, always there. Hebrews 13:5 reads, *"I will never leave you, nor forsake you."* In the original Hebrew, the word *never* is a five-negative word. It would translate like this, "I will never, never, never, never, never leave you nor forsake you."

It's almost as if God is saying to us, "Are you getting it? I really mean it. My care and presence is always there."

What in life can come our way that God can't handle or would separate us from Him? In Romans 8:28-38 we are reminded that nothing can separate us from God and we can be conquerors. *"And we know that in all things God works for the good* (to bring about what is good) *of those who love Him. What, then, shall we say in response to this? If God is for us,* (God can be trusted) *who can be against us? He who did not spare His own Son, but gave Him up for us all—how will He not also, along with Him, graciously give us all things? Who will bring any charge against those whom God has chosen? It is God who justifies. Who is he that condemns? Christ Jesus who died—more than that, who was raised to life—is at the right hand of God and is also interceding for us. Who shall separate us from the love of Christ? Shall trouble or hardship or persecution or famine or nakedness or danger or sword? As it is written: For your sake we face death all day long; We are considered as sheep to be slaughtered."*

"No, in all these things we are more than conquerors through Him who loved us. For I am convinced that neither death nor life, neither angels nor demons, neither the present nor the future, nor any powers, neither height nor depth, nor anything else in all creation, will be able to separate us from the love of God that is in Christ Jesus our Lord."

I'm telling you that God is trustworthy. God loves you. God cares for you and God's care is constant! Believe it. You can have complete reliance on these trust statements.

GOD WANTS TO DO YOU GOOD

Years ago I attended a Billy Graham School of Evangelism. Each day, nearly 500 ministers attended the school. The day's training consisted of keynote speakers as we gathered together to start the day, in addition to classes you could take on evangelism. The teachings and the classes were inspiring relating to the importance of evangelism and the love that God has for this world. We needed to be committed to evangelism and proclaiming the gospel message to the world.

Each morning they would have a guest minister address the conference. On the second day, I was seated in the third row at the end. A black minister was introduced as the morning keynote speaker. Half way through his talk, he drove home a point I have never forgotten. He looked out over all the ministers who had gathered for the conference and simply said the following:

"God wants to do you good. He don't want to do you bad. I tell you again, God wants to do you good, and He don't want to do you bad." He repeated himself four times, and as he did, the one thing that honestly caught my attention was his grammar. "Don't want to do you bad" just didn't sound correct.

Well, he continued to repeat himself that "God wants to do you good. He don't want to do you bad." He then said, "Who told you that God ever wanted to do you bad? Whoever told you that is a liar. They are a LIAR!" and he shouted out the word 'liar'. "I want to talk to them and let them know they are wrong. If you believe that, you are wrong and being deceived."

"Now I am telling you, God wants to do you good. He don't want to do you bad. Do you believe these words?" He paused and seemed to stare at everyone in the audience. As he said those words and stared us all down, it felt like he was talking to and looking directly at me. I was ready to stand up and shout, "I believe, God wants to do me good!!"

Today if you asked me what year I attended that conference, I couldn't tell you. If you asked me the name of the minister who gave that talk, I couldn't tell you to save my life. What I do remember are his words that rang true that day with the power of the Holy Spirit. "God wants to do you good. He don't want to do you bad."

I have never forgotten those words. They have proven to be trustworthy and beneficial to my life. It is written in Matthew 11: 28-30, *"Come unto me all you who are weak and heavy laden and I will give you rest. Take my yoke upon you and learn from me, for I am gentle and humble in heart and you will find rest for your souls. For my yoke is easy and my burden is light."*

A TRUST STATEMENT TO GOD

Trust is an important aspect in knowing God and His will for our life. When one has trust in someone, the relationship is stronger. To trust is a strength that bonds and binds God and you together.

Make a choice right now to trust God, even if you can't understand the "whys" of what you are going through. It's an act of your will through faith and it will enable you to stand firm regardless of how severe the storm of life may become.

Don't try to figure out how God is going to use adversity for good. Trying to discover His ultimate purpose in such circumstances often leads to absurd conclusions or outright despair. Just trust Him. It really is a matter of trust.

Read the following as a trust statement from you to God. Say it as a prayer and a personal word from your heart to God. I hope it adds comfort and strength to you:

"I don't always understand the situations and circumstances of my life, but I am willing to trust in you, God."

"Trust in the Lord with all thy heart, do not lean on your own understanding, in all your ways acknowledge Him and He will make your paths straight." Proverbs 3:5-6.

WHAT ABOUT US?

1. Who in your life would you consider as being trustworthy? Why would you consider them trustworthy?

2. Take a moment to recall the trust statements about God. On a scale of 1 to 10, what number would you put beside each statement concerning you and God, both in your life, and in your belief?

    a) God is trustworthy. _____

    b) God loves you. _____

    c) God cares about you. _____

    d) God's care is constant. _____

    e) God wants to do you good. _____

3. Are there any trust statements that you would add to the list?

CHAPTER SIX

I LOVE YOU LORD

Years ago, I read the account of a lady named Margaret Fishback and the background to a poem she had written. Many of you might not know who Margaret is, yet are familiar with her poem. I was so moved by the story that I want to share it with you.

When Margaret was in her late 20's, she fell deeply in love. The relationship with this man was nothing like any other relationship she had ever been in. The love she felt for him confirmed that he was her true love—the one she would marry. No other man had so moved her. No other man had so touched her heart.

Later that year, this man broke off the relationship with Margaret. He left her and went his own way. Her heart was broken in so many pieces, shattered in a way that she wondered if it could ever be mended. From there, Margaret got sick and was diagnosed with meningitis. For months she spent most of her time in bed, dealing with the sickness and taking a journey down a long road to recovery.

The good news is that she did recover. After her recovery, someone came along who had feelings for her—a love that he wanted to share only with her. The relationship between the two seemed to be progressing very well. Yet the day came when Margaret broke off the relationship. She told him she did not want to see him anymore; that she felt in her heart the relationship needed to come to an end.

The following week, a close friend of hers asked, "Margaret, why did you break up with this man?" She really thought the two of them had a good thing going. The break-up made no sense at all to Margaret's friend. Margaret looked at her friend and replied, "I'm all out of trust. I'm not even sure I can trust

God. I know for sure that I can't trust another man. I am totally out of trust. Without trust, I can't be in any kind of relationship."

In the months to come, Margaret wrestled with the questions about her life and all she had gone through the past few years. The questions were difficult and there were no answers that were sufficient or made sense. Depression and loneliness consumed many hours of her life.

It was at this point in her life that Margaret took out a pen and piece of paper and wrote down her feelings about her life and God. This particular night, she sat by herself and wrote as honestly as she could about her questions, doubts, and feelings. Many of her words and thoughts seemed negative relating to her life and her relationship with God. Yet, they were honest and helped lead her to an understanding of her life, what she had been through, and how God was still an active part of it. Yes, God was still a part of it, even if her relationship with Him seemed silent and still.

She wrote her thoughts and feelings in the form of a poem that touched her deeply. The words in the poem spoke truth in a way that encouraged her from this moment in her life through her journey to understanding and recovery. The words of her poem have been published and read by so many to bring encouragement and hope. Here is her moving poem, written in solitude from a point in her life that was so difficult and hard to understand. You've probably heard of it.

Footprints In the Sand

One night I dreamed a dream. I was walking along the beach with my Lord. Across the dark sky flashed scenes from my life. For each scene, I noticed two sets of footprints in the sand, one belonging to me and one to my Lord.

When the last scene of my life shot before me, I looked back at the footprints in the sand. There was only one set of footprints. I realized that this was at the lowest and saddest times of my life. This always bothered me and I questioned the Lord about my dilemma.

"Lord, You told me when I decided to follow You, You would walk and talk with me all the way. But I'm aware that during the most troublesome times of my life, there is only one set of footprints. I just don't understand why, when I need You most, You leave me."

He whispered, "My precious child, I love you and will never leave you, never, ever, during your trials and testings. When you saw only one set of footprints, it was then that I carried you."

I LOVE YOU, LORD

When we talk about who's got your back, I believe that God truly does have our backs. Like the thoughts in "Footprints in the Sand," we might not always be able to attest to His presence and concern. Yet, that doesn't mean He doesn't have our backs and concern in His mind for us. God loves us and will never leave nor forsake us.

While in the service and fighting in the war, I learned so much about God and his love for me. These truths have stayed with me all these years and have proven to be of immense value, strength, hope and encouragement. My relationship with God is the most significant aspect of my life. I want to share with you four truths about God that strengthened me back then, and have remained with me. They speak loudly to the fact that God has our backs. The four truths are:

1. A personal love and relationship with God;

2. The value of the word of God;

3. The privilege and need of prayer;

4. The Lordship of Christ.

In this chapter, I want to talk about our love for God. The chapters that follow will deal with more of the truths. I pray these chapters will strengthen your relationship with God. I pray your love for God will grow in fresh meaningful ways. I hope you will sense and see His footprints in the sand as it relates to you and your life.

LEAVING HOME

After seven months, I completed all the training required to be an infantry soldier. The training was long, difficult and challenging. It served its purpose very well. I graduated with a confidence that would now be put to the real test as I prepared to go off to war.

I returned home for two weeks of R&R (rest and relaxation). Talk about time not cooperating. Those two weeks flew by so fast! I did as much living as possible in that short period of time. My time was spent with friends and family, and it seemed like every hour of every day was taken up with someone or something to do.

It was all very meaningful and important. All the things I did with my friends during those two weeks were not anything new. Yet, it all felt so good and wonderful as I experienced it. From hanging out, to playing basketball, to getting our favorite hamburgers, to just talking. Those days with my friends were days I will always cherish and appreciate so much.

I also spent time with my family. Of course, mom made me some of my favorite foods. The aroma of the food cooking penetrated the entire house. I could smell the food cooking and absorbed this wonderful moment. My mom is truly a great cook. We sat around and had dinner together. We talked, laughed and enjoyed our time together as a family.

At night, I slept in my own bed. Talk about comfort and sleeping on a cloud. I truly rested for hours like I hadn't in quite some time. The bed and my bedroom were truly a sanctuary of peace, comfort and rest. I would lie there with some music playing on the stereo, contemplating my life and the days that were ahead for me. Finally, I would roll over, tuck my hand under the pillow and drift off into a peaceful and restful sleep.

Before I knew it, the two weeks had passed. The morning arrived when I would again have to leave my home in Glendale, California. The scenario played out in my mind. I would take a drive to Los Angeles International Airport (LAX) where I would board a jet that would fly me to Seattle. I would then be driven to the army base Fort Lewis. There I would spend three days of final processing. On the fourth day, I would board another jet that would fly me from Seattle to Vietnam.

I left my bedroom and went to the den to say goodbye to mom. My dad was in the car waiting to drive me to the airport. My mom would not (actually, could not) accompany us to the airport. As a mom, she just found it too hard to take that drive with me. We talked a few minutes, shed some tears together, and hugged (I mean, really hugged) each other. This was a tough moment for both of us. I love my mom. She was always a good mom to my brother and me. Now, we had to say goodbye, not knowing if we would ever see each other again.

The drive from my house to the airport takes one hour. I quietly gazed out the window as my father drove the car. He paid close attention to his driving, not speaking one word to me. He just kept his eyes on the road as we got closer and closer to the airport with each minute that passed. I wondered what he was thinking. What was going through his head as he silently sat there driving me to a destination that would take me to Vietnam? It wasn't long before those questions were answered.

We arrived at the airport and I got my ticket at the airline counter. My dad and I walked together to the boarding gate. In those days, family or friends could walk together to the airplane and say their goodbyes. (Since the incident on 9/11, those days of family and friends walking each other to the airplane are gone!)

When we got to the gate, we strolled over to those huge windows where people can watch the planes taking off and landing. We stood there and observed the 737 jet that was parked at the gate. In a few minutes, I would be boarding that jet and it would take me on to Seattle.

Our silence was interrupted by a message over the intercom, "Flight 107 for Seattle is now ready to board." At that moment my dad turned and spoke to me for the first time since we left the house. He softly said to me, "You do not have to leave yet. You still have time to board. They will call at least two more times."

He then turned back towards the window and continued to stare at the jet. I turned to look at my father. I saw something I will never forget. Tears were flowing down his face. My dad was crying.

Suddenly, again over the intercom came that same announcement, "Flight 107 for Seattle is now boarding."

Again, dad responded by saying, "Not yet. They will call a third time." So we stood there, father and son, for a few more precious moments.

Then the third announcement came, "This is the final boarding call for flight 107 for Seattle. All ticketed passengers must be on board."

My dad turned and looked at me. He said, "Son, I love you and I'm going to miss you. Right now I'm hurting as a father because I don't want you to go. One day you will be a father and will know how a moment like this hurts. I love you, Michael. I don't want you to leave, but I know you must." He reached out, hugged me, gave me a kiss and said, "I'll see you again and I am praying for you."

I hugged my dad with an embrace that said, "I love you too, and I am so fortunate to have you as my dad." The embrace lasted for well over a minute. I boarded the jet with tears in my eyes. For the entire flight to Seattle, I didn't say a word to anyone. All I could do was think of my father's face, his tears, and the words he had spoken to me.

Now, some might think that perhaps at this particular time in my life, my dad should have been a bit stronger. After all, I was the one going to war, not him. At this time, wouldn't I have needed a stronger dad who could look at me and say, "Son, it's going to be okay. Trust in God. We are behind you and don't worry. Everything will be alright."

But dad had not been able to say that because he was hurting too, and he had risked himself by being open and honest. He allowed me to share in his own hurt even as he continued to share in mine. That exchange of honest love and caring created a wonderful bond between my father and me. Words are inadequate to describe its strength, even to this day.

MY TRIP TO VIETNAM

I arrived in Seattle, and was there for three days. When I had moments alone, I would find myself thinking about my life and all that had transpired in the past year. I recalled the previous year when I had rededicated my life to God. It truly was a meaningful time in my life. At that same time, my girlfriend, the one I thought I would marry, broke up with me. That seemed like more than I could handle. Then, I received my draft notice. Shortly thereafter, I received my orders to be an infantry soldier, which would take me to Vietnam.

Since I had just left my mom at home in tears, and my dad at the airport hurting and in tears, I began to wonder, "Is this truly the abundant life in God? If this is the abundant life, I really don't want to know what the non-abundant life without God is like." This truly was not a wonderful abundant scenario, according to my way of thinking.

During my entire stay in Seattle, I continued to think about my relationship with God. I found I was becoming more and more angry and upset at Him. It seemed that things got worse ever since I had given my life over to Him. My desire to grow and my commitment to live a lifestyle in Jesus Christ were real. Since I had given my life to Jesus in sincerity, I should not be on this jet bound for Vietnam! What my family was going through at home was not for the best. It was not fair and I was definitely angry.

I remember boarding the plane that would take me to Vietnam. I sat alone, angry inside and frightened, even with 200 other soldiers on board. There would be one brief stop in the Philippines for fuel. We would then proceed to Vietnam. On the last part of the flight, just after leaving the Philippines, I felt the Lord responding to my needs and I felt Him wanting to help me deal with my anger, frustrations and questions.

In my heart and in my mind, I heard these words spoken to me as clearly as if God was sitting in the seat beside me, "Michael, I know that you are angry and confused. I know you are mad at me. Michael, I want to ask you a question. Can't the God that I am, the powerful God, the caring God that you have fallen in love with in Glendale, be the same powerful and caring God in Vietnam? Is my love and power and my caring confined to the boundaries of California? Will I be with you, even though you are not in California?"

These were difficult questions. Honestly, I didn't answer them at that time. I was so angry, hurt and confused, that I refused to listen to God. "Just leave me alone and let me be!" The questions stayed in my mind, yet silence came from within me. For the next hour on the flight, I just sat there. Finally, the jet made its final approach to land and within the next few hours, all the questions would be answered.

THE BIG, SCARY SERGEANT

At a very slow pace, 200 men and women began to step down from the jet. We assembled into formation 500 yards away. There I was, standing in formation on the runway. The air was hot and humid. Sweat began to pour from my skin. In the distance, I heard bombs exploding. Overhead flew two helicopters that were bringing in wounded soldiers. Fighter jets took off from a distant runway. This all took place within five minutes of exiting the jet! It was really happening. I was in the middle of a war zone, far away from home.

In the distance, I observed an army sergeant making his way towards us. I watched as he got closer and closer to us. I was amazed at how very muscular he was. In fact, he had muscles in places where I didn't even have places! Sweat was pouring down from his head and he walked tough, with steps of determination.

He was walking towards us. He was wearing an American army uniform and he was putting fear into me like no one has ever done before. I was terrified just looking at him, and he wasn't even the enemy. He was one of us!

He stopped in front of the formation and stared at us for what seemed an eternity. After looking us all over, he said. "Welcome to Vietnam, the land of opportunity. How many of you do not believe in God? Raise your hands." Well, maybe 10-15 hands went up. He looked them over and then simply stated. "I have news for you. Within one month, each one of you will believe. Have a good day."

He then turned and walked away into the distance. I know he probably said a few additional words, but that was the part of the conversation that I heard and remember. Three hours later, I found myself with some free time, so I decided to go and get a Pepsi. As I was walking towards the building to get a drink, guess who was walking out of the building heading right towards me? Yes, you guessed it. The big, muscular, mean, sweaty sergeant. Coming right at me!

Somehow, I got the nerve to stop and speak to him. I said, "Sergeant, this is my first day in Vietnam and I just heard your welcome speech a few hours ago on the runway. You're a Christian?" He nodded, yes. I said, "Well, I'm a Christian too, and I am mad at God and scared." He looked me right in the eyes and said, "Hey private, He is never going to leave you nor forsake you. Now you have a good day." And with that, he walked away into the distance again.

For the record, I do not believe this man was human. I believe he was an angel, put there by God, ministering to the soldiers. I believe in angels and that they are ministering agents for God to us. Remember the television show *Touched By An Angel?* Well, this was one of the angels that truly existed. They could have made an episode on that show about this guy!

I got my Pepsi and found a place to sit by myself. For the first time in four days, I looked up and talked to God. I said, "I don't get it, God. I'm confused and scared. I want to cry and go home." Once again I heard that voice within my heart and mind. "Michael, you are going to have to answer these questions: Is the God you love and who you think cares for you, the same God here in Vietnam as He was in California? Am I still your God and are you my man?"

This time I answered the question. "Yes, you are my God and I am your man. Whether I understand or not, no matter what I am feeling, you will never leave me nor forsake me. I will do all things through Christ who strengthens me. I love you Lord." And the last words I heard back were, "I love you Michael. Now, on to war."

My walk with God continued throughout the months of my tour of duty in Vietnam. The relationship grew stronger and stronger and has remained, long after I was discharged from the army.

A LETTER TO MOM

There are two other stories I want to share with you about God and me that took place that year in Vietnam. One has to do with a letter I received from my mom. In her letter, she shared the typical news about home and what was going on with my family and friends. She told me that she prays for me each and every day. She also shared how much she missed me and that she had cried many tears for me.

I could tell by her words that she was truly hurting. So, I sat down one afternoon and wrote her a letter back. Part of the letter read, "Mom, I know how much you love me and miss me. Your love as my mom has always been there. I know you are scared inside and concerned for me. Mom, I want to share something with you that I really want you to hear and understand. There isn't a bullet or bomb that can ever kill your son. There are bullets that can hurt me or take me from this world. But, there is no bullet that could ever kill me. I have eternal life in Jesus Christ. I believe that with all my heart. Where there is eternal life, you cannot have death. The two do not go together."

The letter continued, "Now mom, I don't want to die. I want to come home to you and dad. I want to eat your cooking. You are a fantastic cook and there is nothing I want more than to sit down to dinner with both of you again. I look forward to the day when we will meet at the airport and hug each other again. Until then, take these words of hope and comfort to your side. I have eternal life. You cannot have death, where there is eternal life. John 3:16 is a true scripture. See you in six months. I love you, mom!"

When my mom received this letter, it helped bring some comfort to her. In fact, she told me she has never thrown that letter away. She keeps it and remembers the promises of God that are contained within it.

A LIGHT IN THE SKY

After four months in Vietnam, I was assigned to a special mission along with eight other men. We were to go into different villages and teach their soldiers how to defend themselves and their families against the enemy. We would spend two to four weeks at one village, then we would move on to the next village. After a while, we would repeat our training back at the first village. Because of this special assignment, I spent an average of four or five nights each week on ambush, defending the village from attacks by the enemy. There were always the nine of us, along with 20-25 Vietnamese soldiers.

I will never forget one ambush that took place during my ninth month that proved to be life changing. We left the village as the sun began to set, as we did with any other ambush. The 30 of us walked towards the site where we would set up our defense for the evening. Three men walked point, 20 yards ahead of the rest of us.

As we got near our ambush site, the point men encountered enemy fire. They fell to the ground, as did the rest of us. We remained silent and tried to determine where the gunfire was coming from. The gunfire ceased and we held our position for the next 30 minutes.

We then received an intelligence report that there was possibly a company of enemy soldiers moving through this sector. A company of soldiers can be anywhere from 100 to 200 in size.

We informed our firebase that we were not going to proceed further to our assigned ambush site, but would set up the ambush right where we were. We did not want to risk walking into one of their ambushes.

As one of the leaders, I informed each soldier of the plan for the evening. We set up the ambush in groups of three. On a typical ambush, everyone stays awake and alert until midnight, then from midnight to 6 a.m., two-hour shifts are taken at each site. One person stays up until 2 a.m. while his two buddies try to get some sleep. At 2 a.m. you wake up a buddy for his shift, then you get some sleep. At 4 a.m. the last buddy is awaken for his turn. Then, hopefully at 6 a.m. you see one of the most beautiful sights in the world -- the sun is rising and you've survived another night in the jungle. Sunrises have incredibly deep meaning to soldiers. Another day has passed.

At about 9 p.m. that night, one of our helicopters flew above our position. I got in contact with the pilot and asked if he could make a few passes to see if he could spot any movement. He informed me that he would.

It was on his second go around that I heard him say, "Uh oh." Now those are not the words you want to hear when formed together. Look it up in the dictionary. "Oh" means something is wrong. The "uh" part is equally as bad. He then informed me that he had spotted two flashlights in the jungle. I then replied back to him. "Uh oh."

Flashlights could mean that the enemy was setting the sites on some of their bombs. They could be getting ready for combat. I thanked the pilot for the information and his assistance. He said, "God be with you," as he flew from our sight. I informed everyone of my conversation and told them to prepare for battle. Because of this information, no one would sleep tonight. Everyone would stay awake and be ready to do battle.

Hours passed and nothing happened. I was getting tired, so I reached into my pocket and took out a piece of Double-Mint gum. I unwrapped it, put it into my mouth and hoped that it would help me stay awake. As I chewed the gum, I kept looking for movement, but nothing moved in the silent jungle.

It was a little after midnight when something in my brain told me to look up into the sky. As I did, I noticed flashing lights silently moving across the sky. From the direction the lights were traveling, I could tell that the lights were on the end of the wing of a jetliner. I could also determine from the direction the lights were traveling, that the jet was headed towards the United States.

I continued to stare at the lights until they began to disappear into the blackness of the night. As they were almost out of sight, I wanted to reach out and grab them. I did not want them to leave. Those lights stood for everything I wanted that night. Those lights stood for home. Those lights stood for my family. No more war. No more being shot at. I wanted to be on that jet. I did not want to spend one more night in the jungle. I'd had enough of this!

The lights disappeared into the darkness, and there I remained in the jungle. About an hour later, I did something no one should ever do in war. I took my weapon from my hand and laid it down on the ground. A soldier never lets go of his weapon. As it rested on the ground, I reached into my pocket and next to my pack of gum was my pocket version of the Bible's New Testament. I took the Bible from my pocket and stared at it. I held it in my hand and felt it like never before. I then looked up into the sky and said the following prayer: "God, if you let me live and if you help me understand this book, I will speak for you." That was my prayer. It was not long, fancy or drawn out. I repeated it three times.

I don't honestly know why those particular words came out of my mouth. I had no thoughts of being a minister. In fact, I wanted to be a probation officer. I wasn't the greatest Christian. In school, one of my biggest fears was public speaking. I just wasn't comfortable speaking in front of people. Now, here I was, in the middle of the jungle saying this prayer, which truly made little sense to me and who I was at this particular time in my life.

Well, 6 a.m. arrived and the sun began to rise. I told everyone to unload (shoot) a clip of ammunition into the jungle. On the count of three, all 30 of us fired our weapons. Branches were breaking and pieces of trees were falling to the ground as the shots pierced the air. Birds were flying for safety out of the trees. Then silence. We waited five minutes and no fire was returned. We then got up and returned to the village.

The following week, another group of soldiers were in that same general vicinity. The enemy encountered them. The bombs across their position killed nearly half of them. Thank God, nothing like that had happened to us.

THE LIGHTS AGAIN

Three months later, I found myself in the city of Cam Rahn Bay, Vietnam. I had served my wartime obligation for one year and now I was going home. This was the main city in Vietnam where our commercial jets would land to take our soldiers who had done their time home. I was so fortunate. I had survived without injury. I was going home! I got my seat assignment and proceeded to the plane along with 200 other soldiers.

As I boarded the plane, I walked up the aisle, looking for my seat. When I got to it, I noticed I had a window seat. I sat down, buckled my seat belt and thought to myself, "Start the engines, get this plane in the air, and let's go home!"

While I was having this thought, something in my brain told me to look out the window. I turned and noticed that not only did I have a window seat, but I had a window seat overlooking the wing of the jetliner. As I looked out the window, there at the end of the wing were the flashing lights. The same red and white lights I saw three months ago while on ambush. I couldn't take my eyes off the lights. I continued to stare at them, as if they were flashing just for me.

Ten minutes later, the door of the jet was closed. We taxied to the end of the runway. You would have thought that there would be a lot of chatter and conversation going on within the plane, but there was little. Everyone just sat quietly in their seats, keeping to themselves.

After a few moments, you could hear and feel the power of the jet engines as the pilot began to increase their thrust. He then released the brake and the jet began its journey down the runway. It picked up speed, and more speed, until that one moment when there was sufficient speed that the nose of the jet and its wheels left the ground.

It was at that moment, when the plane left the ground, 200 men and women screamed, cheered and many cried. We are going home!! We made it. No more war! No more bombs and bullets. We are fortunate. We served our time and now we are going home.

The jetliner made a complete circle around the airport. Looking below, it was completely dark. Amazing. A war zone and no lights to be seen. The plane leveled off and headed on course for the United States. I sat in my seat and continued to stare at the flashing lights at the end of the wing.

Several minutes later, I looked above into the sky and said a prayer: "God, I prayed three months ago that if you would let me live and help me understand the Bible, I would speak for you. I made you that promise. I have no idea what that means, but I gave you my word."

I returned to California for 30 days of R&R and then would have to report to Fort Hood, Texas, for my final three months of service. I had been home barely one week when I received a call from a minister who told me of a high school camp that would take place the following week. He asked if I would be able to attend one evening and give my testimony. He told me there would be 400 young people at the camp and again asked if I would be available.

I told him that I would be available. Five days later I found myself speaking to 400 young people about my love for and journey with God. Many years have passed since that speaking engagement. I feel the need to share with you the two most important things about Mike Slater.

First of all, I am deeply in love with Jesus Christ. I do not tell you that as a minister. I tell you that as a man, son, husband, dad and friend. I am deeply in love with Jesus Christ. Years ago, I surrendered my life to God, and it's the best decision I have ever made.

Secondly, years ago I made a promise to God in the jungles of Vietnam. "Let me live and help me understand the Bible and I will speak for you." I have never broken that promise to God, "Let me live and help me understand Your Word and I will speak for you, wherever that may be."

ONLY A CHORUS

I found myself speaking at a conference to young adults in the Santa Cruz Mountains of California. On the second evening that I was supposed to speak, I made my way to the auditorium, found my seat and sat down to listen to the time of worship that preceded my talk. Different songs were sung that created an atmosphere of worship and praise to God. The last song was a chorus that I had heard once before. It was only a short chorus, simple words, yet this evening I listened and experienced it in a way that moved me to tears. The chorus was this familiar tune:

I love you, Lord
And I lift my voice
To worship You, oh my soul rejoice.

Take joy my King
In what You hear
May it be a sweet, sweet sound to Your ears.

The chorus was sung softly. After singing it through once, it was repeated. Over and over again it was sung. It seemed that the chorus was being sung not only as a group, but also as individuals to God. The whole focus of the words and the singing was each person individually singing it from their heart to God. No one else mattered at that moment.

Towards the end, the intensity and conviction of the chorus rang out throughout the auditorium. I sat there so moved by the expression of love that these young adults had for God. It moved me to tears and I cried out to God that I wanted to love Him as deeply as what I felt was taking place in this auditorium. I wanted God to know how deeply I loved Him, and that I wanted my life to be a sweet, sweet sound to His ears.

Somehow, I made it through the talk. Later that night, I was having a milkshake with two of the leaders and expressed to them what I felt in that auditorium that evening. There was a love that seemed to be so sincere from many of the young adults.

One of the leaders then began to share with me some of the backgrounds of many of the people who were attending this conference. They were an ethnic group of young adults. Their families had disowned many of them because of their conviction and relationship with Jesus. Support for their education and future had been cut off. Their choice to follow Jesus truly had proven costly. Yet they sang, believed, and would not turn from their love of God.

I sat there thinking about my love for God. How deep, personal and solid was it? Could those words truly be sung from my heart with love for God, conviction and truth? Later in the evening, walking alone in those mountains, I again answered, "Yes Lord. I love you and want my life to be a sweet sound to your ears."

That chorus has remained with me for years. It is only a chorus, simple yet so true. I am asking you now about your love for God. Have you given your life over to Jesus? Is He truly your savior and Lord? Can you sing from your heart, "I love you Lord and I lift up my voice?"

Billy Graham, a great man of God and exceptional evangelist of our time, always gives an altar call at the end of his messages for those who choose to accept Christ into their lives. His altar call always includes the same statement. He asks if you are willing to "surrender your life to Jesus" right now. He always uses the word "surrender".

I believe the word surrender is a beautiful word that we need to truly understand. When you surrender to someone, it means you are in their hands. You are giving up your rights and powers over to that person. You are in their custody. They have the power over you.

I'm asking you what I have asked so many people about surrendering their life to God. Is it worth having your life in the hands of God? Are those hands and His power over you beneficial or not? Is it worthwhile to you as a person and for your life to be in the Lord's hold? Have you surrendered your life completely over to God? Have you asked Him into your life? You can answer, "yes" right now and give your life over to Him.

THE LORD IS MY SHEPHERD

There is a beautiful portion of scripture called the 23rd Psalm. In a survey about the Bible, people were asked what their favorite and most remembered portion of scripture was. The findings of the survey showed John 3:16 as the second most popular and known scripture. The 23rd Psalm was the most popular and known of all the scripture in the Bible.

Now, the 23rd Psalm is a story of a relationship between God and his people. The analogy used is of a shepherd and his sheep. The shepherd is God, and the sheep represent people like you and me.

It depicts the life of a shepherd and his sheep for one year. All that can be experienced that year is summarized in the Psalm. The ups and downs, the challenges, the seasons of good and want, are all expressed in the Psalm. It talks about life's journey for the sheep and their shepherd. There is no separating the two.

The love relationship the shepherd has for his sheep is stated so beautifully.

The Psalm contains only 118 words. That's not very long. In fact, many people have memorized this portion of scripture. It consists of short phrases. The phrases speak to a particular aspect of the sheep's life. It could speak of great times like lying down in green pastures. Or one of concern and fear, like walking through the valley of the shadow of death. Those times of life that are difficult and challenging for us are our valleys.

The Psalm speaks of a confidence in God. It speaks of hope for all aspects of one's life. A faith approach to life based on a personal relationship with God.

Now the power and the meaning of the Psalm can be found in the first five words. If one does not believe in the first five words, the 113 that follow hold little if any meaning. The first five words are, "The Lord is my shepherd." There it is, so simple, yet it holds all the meaning and truth for us. Five words, spoken as a calm statement of fact. Five words spoken in full allegiance and surrender to God.

One has to believe and personally accept the first five words for the following 113 words to make sense and prove true. The Lord is my shepherd. This is an individual decision, not based on or through anyone else. The choice has to be made by each one of us.

WHAT ABOUT US?

1. What about God and you? Where do you stand concerning Jesus as your savior and Lord? Have you asked Jesus into your life? Do you have a personal relationship with Jesus?

   Have you surrendered your life to God? Do you believe His hands are good hands for your life to be in? Can you truly say, "The Lord is my shepherd?" Can you live in a position of confidence, hope and faith-approach to life? To know the shepherd is to know the Psalm. It's the relationship with the shepherd that gives meaning to the words of the Psalm.

2. As you think about your life, its challenges, and its demands, I hope you realize that God does care for you and He has your back. Can you recall any of those times? Through my years in the service and my time in the jungles of Vietnam, I realized He still cared for me and had my back, despite my confusion and anger. And he still has my back to this very day.

3. God loves you. Take a moment to look down at your feet. As you do, try to visualize two sets of footprints, yours and God's. The footprints you make in life are never on your own. If you only see one set, my friend, it just might be that God is lifting and carrying you. He is never going to leave you. He just won't do that.

4. *God loves you*. Don't let anyone or anything dissuade you of that fact. Now, say back to Him, "I love you Lord. I love you Lord." Tell Him you love Him. Speak those words or sing those words. "I love you Lord." Let God hear those words come from your lips. May you in turn and hear His words to you, "I love you."

CHAPTER SEVEN

THE WORD OF GOD

In a previous chapter, I told you about the first truth I learned. The second truth I learned was the value of the word of God. Words written that would impact my life in ways that I never dreamed possible. Words written that would forever remain with me. A book called the Bible that would become so precious to me that I would carry it with me the rest of my life.

When I entered the service, I took my personal Bible and a pocket New Testament that someone had given me as a gift. I got my personal Bible when I was 11 years old for my birthday. Here I was 21 years old and I still had that very Bible.

I wish I could tell you that I read the Bible every day and that it was worn out. Well, I did read it once in awhile and took it to church every Sunday that I attended. During the week, it remained on my desk. That was a safe place for my Bible and never once did I lose it.

In church, I listened to many messages and turned to many passages in the Bible. It was during my high school years that the word of God began to have some meaning. Not real deep, but something was happening to me as I listened to the Word and began to read it more.

It was in the service, not in a church or Sunday school class, when the value of the word of God truly came forth. Remember how I told you those first few months in the army were scary and lonely? Well, the word of God began to deal with that and counteract all that negative stuff I was feeling.

I got in the habit of reading the Bible in the barracks each night before I went to bed. Alone on my bunk, I would read passages of scripture. Most of my reading was from the New Testament. As I read, the words felt comforting and began to speak to me. It was the same Bible that I'd had for years, yet now it seemed to speak to me in a very personal and special way.

In the mornings, when I went to formation for the day's training, I always left with my pocket New Testament. It was always with me. We'd get breaks periodically throughout the day. We'd stop our training, take a seat right where we were at that particular time, and rest. The sergeant would say, "If you've got one, light it." That meant if you smoked, now was the time to light up and puff away.

As we sat and rested or smoked, I got in the habit of taking out my New Testament and reading from it. It was much better for me than a cigarette. I would lean back on my backpack and just relax while doing a little reading. It really felt good to read the word of God. Many of the words and thoughts seemed to be speaking to me.

OFF TO WAR

When I went to Vietnam, I continued with the Bible reading habits I had formed during my training. The Bible remained part of my life. I carried that pocket New Testament with me everywhere. I continued to read my Bible at night, when we weren't on maneuvers or ambush.

On the evenings that we prepared to go out on ambush, I would make sure my weapon was cleaned and ready. I'd pack all the essentials in my backpack. I'd make sure I knew the plans for that night, and then I'd sit by myself for a quiet moment alone to read the word of God and to pray. In my ritual, the last thing I did before every ambush was to spend time alone with God. This was both reading and talking to Him.

Through all these disciplines, something was happening between the word of God and me. As I continued to read the Word, it began to make so much sense to me. It felt like the words were living inside me and were meant for me. Here, I was not a minister or the greatest Bible reader or scholar, but some- how I understood the words and the truth of the Bible.

The more I read the word of God, the more it gave me comfort. You could call it more of a peaceful feeling. It was a peace and comfort that filled my body and mind. I had never felt the peace of God like that. It was a peace that surpassed all understanding. The word of God said it was possible and here I was experiencing it.

The word of God was also giving me wisdom. Wisdom meant truth for living. It had little to do with intelligence. The word of God had the knowledge I needed for what I was feeling and dealing with. The word of God was speaking to me and offering the help and insight that I desperately needed.

Next, I was gaining strength from the word of God. My weaknesses, doubts, and fears were being balanced and neutralized by God's word. I began to feel more confident as a person and stronger about my relationship with God. I began to understand what Paul had said in Philippians 4:13, *"I can do all things through Christ which strengthens me."* This was a truth that I could live out, just as Paul had.

The passage, *"Thy word will be a lamp unto my feet and a light unto my path"* proved very true. I was walking stronger in God, with the assurance of not walking alone. I was experiencing the word of God for myself. The confidence and strength were not of my own ability, but from God and His words that were being spoken to me from the Bible.

PRISONER OF WAR

When one is on ambush all night, the hours go by very, very slowly. Something must fill those hours as you wait for a possible enemy encounter. Besides keeping alert and looking out for the enemy, other things tend to take up the hours. You find yourself doing a lot of thinking. Thinking of home and wondering what others are doing right now. In your mind, you picture the people and places you long for.

You can take time to hum some songs to yourself. Songs you grew up with that bring back memories of times gone by. Songs that make you real realize the good times. Even if you didn't remember all the words of the song, you could make up your own. No one had to know because you were only humming the words anyway.

Sometimes you would talk in a whisper to a comrade who was next to you. It's amazing how much discussion can take place with relatively few words on an ambush. It's not totally quiet for the duration of the operation. It's very interesting to find how much you learn about someone and how much one can share during those times of few words.

There were also those other thoughts we all had while time was slowly passing by. Thoughts like, "Is tonight the night that I will come in contact with the enemy? Will there be gunfire? Will I get wounded or killed—or even worse, will I have to kill someone? What if I get captured and become a prisoner of war? What if that happens to me?" After all, many of our soldiers were taken as prisoners of war.

I thought of what the enemy might do to me if I were captured. I knew they would take my weapon from me, as well as anything I had that was personal. I realized that would include my pocket New Testament. Surely, they wouldn't want me to have the Bible. I knew I would be marched off to a POW camp with absolutely no personal possessions.

As I continued to think about this scenario happening to me, I thought of the enemy not so much taking my weapon or my gear, but my pocket New Testament. That truly bothered me, for the word of God meant confidence, strength and wisdom for me. I thought to myself, "Take everything I have, but let me keep my Bible!"

Then it hit me like a ton of bricks! While they could take my pocket New Testament from me, they could *never* take the word of God that I have deep within my heart and mind. Those words I had read often to myself, or had heard others speak in church. Those words I had memorized.

Many nights on ambush I played my own little mind-game of how many scriptures I could quote. How many could I remember and recite without opening my bible? They began to flow from my heart and mind onto my lips. I began to speak the words of John 3:16, Psalm 23, Romans 8:28 and Philippians 4:13. There were so many that I knew not only the words but also where they were found in the Bible. For many that I quoted, I knew the words but was not quite sure of its exact location. I would say the words of the scripture and think, "That's somewhere is the book of James." I'd recall another, and think, "That's somewhere in the book of John".

I realized with joy in my heart, that if I was taken a prisoner of war, the enemy could take my weapon and personal possessions. But most important was knowing that even if they took my pocket New Testament, they could not take from me the word of God that was planted deep within my heart and mind. It would remain with me wherever I went. It would always be my source of strength, wisdom and peace. No one could ever take the word of God from me.

A LIGHT UNTO MY PATH

When we talk about "Who's Got Your Back," the word of God rings out positively with a *"Yes!"* God's word can impact our life, guide us, comfort us and give us wisdom and truth for living. There is a wonderful scripture that speaks of the truth of God's word during our challenges and along our journey. The scripture is Psalm 119:105, *"Your word is a lamp unto my feet and a light unto my path."*

God cares about us, and through His word, offers us wisdom and guidance. He has our back through His word. We need to know the word of God. Each one of us needs to be committed to the faithful intake of scripture. Faithful in this context means "consistent."

At one time in His ministry, Jesus declared to those who believed in Him, which you will find in John 8:31, *"If you continue in my word, you are my disciples indeed."* The key word in that statement is "continue". It means to practice and obey God's word every day. Jesus encouraged each of His followers to do this.

HOW CAN WE GET TO KNOW THE BIBLE?

God's word teaches us that we can get into the scripture in a number of ways. The following are the five means of intake of the word of God. These five means can prove to be of tremendous value and inspiration to each one of us. Judge for yourself how strong you are in each of the five ways of taking in the word of God.

1. Hearing the Word of God.

"Consequently, faith comes from hearing the message and the message is heard through the word of Christ." Romans 10:17

Hearing the word of God spoken weekly is so important. Where do we listen to the word of God spoken?

Where can we *hear* the word of God? Some examples of where you can hear God's word in your life are at church, on the radio, on television, during family talks, at your Bible Study, on CD's, and at Sunday school.

Where do *you* hear the word of God? Thinking about your life, list the places that you hear the word of God.

2. Reading the Word of God

"Blessed is the one who reads the words of this prophecy, and blessed are those who hear it and take it to heart what is written in it, because the time is near." Revelation 1:3

Where are you reading the word of God? When are you reading the word of God? How often do you read your Bible? It has been said that reading is becoming a lost art.

3. Studying the Word of God

"Now the Bereans were of noble character than the Thessalonians, for they received the message with great eagerness and examined the scriptures everyday to see if what Paul said was true." Acts 17:11

We need to take the time daily not only to read the Bible, but also to put some study behind our reading. We need to examine portions of scripture for the truth, meaning and application to our lives.

While studying on your own is good and necessary, it is amazing how your study will be enhanced when you become part of a Bible study group. You'll find new depth when the word of God is taught to a group and time is given for interaction, discussion and understanding of the scriptures. I'd encourage everyone to put in their own personal times of study of the Bible, as well as becoming involved in a Bible study group. Both are so beneficial.

Here are some important characteristics that benefit the study of the Bible.

a.　Bible study must be consistent;
b.　Bible study must be systematic (Have a plan);
c.　Bible study should contain original investigation;
d.　Bible study must have application to daily living.

4. Memorization of Scripture

The scriptures are full of passages that indicate that God wants us to saturate our lives with His word. Both the Old and the New Testaments emphasize a relationship to God's word that can only come through scripture memorization. It is also a fact that Satan does not want us to memorize God's word and will bring a variety of excuses to mind. Ultimately, it's a matter of what our priorities are going to be.

The following lists some advantages of memorizing the word of God and some of the benefits that can be gained:

a.　It increases our faith and trust in God.
b.　It helps in our Christian growth
c.　It increases our knowledge of the word of God and builds a doctrinal foundation for our life.
d.　It is profitable for guidance
e.　It helps us meditate of God's word.
f.　It helps us worship God.
g.　It enables us to witness effectively.
h.　It helps us in counseling others.

5. Meditating On the Word of God

The final means of taking in the word of God is through meditation. Meditation is simply reflecting on what you have on your mind. It is the process of turning it over in one's mind. It is the contact with the scriptures to the point that we understand their relationship to us and their application to our daily life.

Once again, meditation is prayerful reflection with a view to understanding and application. It is giving prayerful thought to God's word in your life with the goal of conforming your life to His will. Psalm 1:1-3 is an excellent scripture relating to meditation, *"Blessed is the man who does not walk in the counsel of the wicked or stand in the way of sinners or sit in the seat of mockers. But his delight is in the law of the Lord, and on his law he meditates day and night. He is like a tree planted by streams of water, which yields its fruit in season and whose leaf does not wither. Whatever he does prospers."* Asking these two questions will help you meditate:

1. What is the meaning of this verse based on its content?

2. How should this verse apply to my life?

WHAT ABOUT US?

1. Write out a plan for studying the word of God.

2. Take the time to strengthen your personal plan for hearing the word of God. What could you add to your list?

3. Memorize a scripture this week.

4. Join a Bible study group or help form one.

CHAPTER EIGHT

THE PRIVILEGE AND THE NEED FOR PRAYER

We'd been out on patrol all week, searching the areas around the villages for signs of the enemy. We had spent five exhausting nights on ambush and now returned back to our compound to rest and recuperate for a few days.

As we were sitting around talking, relaxing, and drinking some Pepsi, (and I must confess, after the taste test, I do prefer Pepsi over Coke), one of my buddies asked me the question, "How do you sleep when you're out on ambush?" I remember looking at him somewhat confused and asked him exactly what he meant by that question. How would I know how I sleep if I'm asleep? After all, I'm not awake and taking notice of myself. He proceeded to explain his thoughts, "This is how I picture it, Mike. When it's not your turn to pull the watch, you curl up on the ground like a little baby in the fetal position and peacefully fall asleep. Your hands are under your head like a pillow and you lie there very peacefully. The only thing missing is a pacifier in your mouth."

We all had a good laugh at the image my buddy had of me sleeping on ambush. I do admit, that isn't a very manly image of a soldier in war. However, I pondered his question for some time. After some really deep thinking, I looked him in the eye and said, "You really want to know how I can sleep on ambush? I mean sleep, and sleep well?" He said, "Yes, I'd really like to know how can you sleep like you do . . so quiet and peaceful in the middle of a jungle filled with combat and the enemy. I looked him straight in the eyes and confidently responded with one word, "God."

With a puzzled look on his face, he looked back at me and asked, "What do you mean, God"? I then proceeded to share my testimony of God, my relationship with Him, and my belief in prayer. I told him I do a lot of praying and talking to God before I go out on ambush, and more frequently while I'm part of an ambush. There are times on the ambush when we must be very still for long periods of time. While being still for an hour doesn't feel like much time to get rest, it feels like an eternity when you are required to *be still* and *not move* for fear the enemy will hear you and attack your position. During those times, when rest is essential, I ask the Lord to give me some peace and help me rest. It might only be for an hour or two. I also ask that He make me alert if I need to be.

At times, I felt God talking back to me, saying, "You want this piece of ground to feel like your comfortable bed at home and your feather pillow?" And I would mentally respond, "Yes, Lord, can you help me and answer this prayer?" And I could feel the answer, "Come on Mike, give me something difficult! Lie down my child and rest in my arms and my presence. This ground is as soft and comfortable as your bed. Sleep my child, I've got your back."

So, that's my answer to your question. I can sleep because of my God and my time in prayer with Him. No magic pills, but rather a simple trust and belief in God. I'm continually talking to him in prayer about my situation, and believing He is listening and will respond.

MILITARY SERVICE AND PRAYER

It was during my time in Vietnam that my prayer life took on a personal significance like I have never known. Prayer had been part of my life since I was a child. I would say my prayers before bed. As the years passed, prayer became part of my existence. But honestly, I never grasped the depth, beauty and significance of prayer until I reached the jungles of Vietnam.

That was when my prayer life took on a whole new meaning and intimacy. Never in my life had I talked to God so much. I felt so alone, scared and uncertain. The only one I knew I could talk to was God. I found myself constantly praying. During the day I found myself praying about so many things. At night, my bed became an altar to God. For hours I would talk to Him. I would speak words to Him from deep within my being. I would lie there at times and cry through some of the prayers. I would lie still hoping for answers and reassurance.

For the record, when I would talk to God, I was not speaking out loud so that everyone would think I had lost my mind and was talking to myself. While the majority of my prayer life was internal, or a type of thought-speak, I will admit that at times, my prayers, however brief, would be out loud. I'm sure your know those prayers . . . "God, help me!" or "Oh, Jesus" or "Thank you, Lord."

I began to understand the need for and meaning of prayer. My prayers became a conversation between my God and me. Conversation implies a communication between two or more people. The quality of the conversation depends on the kind of relationship that exists between the two. This can be as impersonal as the relationship between you and the voice that answers the phone when you dial 411. Or it can be as intimate as the relationship between a husband and a wife.

My time of prayer between God and me became intimate. I felt a connection between the two of us. I felt He was concerned for me. The more I prayed and believed in prayer, the closer I felt to God. My life and situations mattered to God. I was not on my own. Talk about affirmation of "Who's Got Your Back." I truly believed (both then and now) that God does have my back. I am one of His sheep, and I am part of His flock. God cares for Mike Slater.

MY LIFE AND PRAYER

In this new prayer life, I began to believe more in God. This belief has remained with me to this day. The habit of talking to God has stayed true to my being. I talk to Him each and every day. Conversations with Him are an essential part of my day. It could be in the office, in my car, or behind my desk as I think of someone. Throughout the day, I converse with God.

There are times when I wake up from a deep sleep late at night. I sense this is a time the Lord is calling me to prayer. I leave my bedroom and quietly go downstairs to the living room. I sit on the couch that overlooks our back yard and gaze at the peacefulness of the trees, grass and flowers, and often times the glow of the moonlight. After this time of peaceful reflection, I enter a time of prayer.

Many words are spoken on behalf of people I love. Sometimes words are spoken on behalf of individuals that I don't even know—friends of people I know or love. It is a time of intercessory prayer. This is a specific prayer on behalf of and for people who come to mind. I believe these are times when God is placing people on my heart so that together we can lift them up. It is a special time of prayer with God, together caring for someone.

Sometimes when I am awakened, I just kneel by the couch and pray, remaining quiet and still before Him, longing to hear words and thoughts from God. This is a time when I listen and allow God the opportunity to speak to me. Other times I'll sit on the couch and remain still, looking out into the garden and listening for his still voice to speak to me. This is time spent tuning in to God and desiring His words for me.

Many times, I kneel in prayer and the words are few. There may be someone or something specific on my mind. At these moments my prayer goes something like this:

"God, you know why I am here, right?"

"Yes I do, Michael."

"You know what I am feeling inside, right?"

"Yes, I know."

Sometimes many words are spoken by not speaking many words. I remain in prayer on my knees, sometimes crying to the Lord, listening and drawing nearer to God.

There are other times that I go for walks with God. I love to walk along the beaches of California, walking for miles and talking to God or singing songs of praise to Him. Sometimes I go for walks in the park or just around the block. These times of walking and talking with God are times of rejuvenation for me in prayer. I guess I just need to walk more often. I encourage you to take walks with God. It will benefit you not only health wise, but spiritually as well.

WHY SHOULD WE PRAY?

Why should we pray? Because that's what you do when you're a Christian. You *should* pray. Nice answer, but there has to be more to it than that. Why should we pray? When do we pray? It was when I was in the Army that I began to get answers to these questions. Let me share with you the five good reasons I learned on why we should pray.

First of all, prayer is fellowship or companionship with God. Prayer affirms a relationship. I am not alone. I needed to believe that in the Army, more than ever in Vietnam, and throughout the years that followed.

Too often, many people feel like a person lost in a crowd or a small voice off in the distance. We are a part of many, yet so impersonal and disconnected. Prayer taught me that I am connected, and that someone does care about me.

Secondly, prayer allows a time of ministering to me. Through my questions, tears, hurts, and fears, no matter what, as I talk with God and get things off my chest, I am being ministered to. Whatever I feel inside, no matter where I'm coming from, God is able to assure me that He cares. I began to understand the verses in Matthew 11:28-3, *"Come unto me all you that are weary and heavy laden and I will give you rest. Take my yoke upon you and learn from me, for I am gentle and humble in heart and you will find rest for your souls. For my yoke is easy and my burden is light."*

God and His spirit were ministering to me. It was a quiet confidence of His presence. It was with this thought that Psalm

23 took on a whole new meaning to me. The Lord *was* my shepherd and I *did not* want. His presence was with me and prayer was affirming that belief.

Thirdly, prayer taught me how to live and how to face my challenges. How to get out of bed each morning and take on another day. I learned how to conquer fears and weaknesses. Prayer gave me insight and truth for living. As stated in Romans 8:28, 31, 35-39, *"And we know that in all things God works for the good of those who love Him. What, then, shall we say in response to this? If God is for us, who can be against us? Who shall separate us from the love of God? Shall trouble or hardship or persecution or famine or nakedness or danger or sword? No, in all these things we are more than conquerors through Him who loved us. For I am convinced that neither death nor life, neither angels nor demons, neither the present nor the future, nor any powers, neither height nor depth, nor anything else in all creation, will be able to separate us from the love of God that is in Christ Jesus our Lord."*

Prayer helps me live day-by-day, week-by-week and month-by-month. I am not just existing or going through the motions. I am a conqueror, living life *with* God and *through* God.

Fourth, the reason I pray is because it gives me strength. There is strength and a power that is not my own. My capabilities are beyond my own abilities. Prayer is adding to my life and not subtracting from it.

I feel more confident after times of prayer. Never do I feel weaker because of the time I spend in prayer. My times in prayer are building me up. Words that come from that special time in prayer are confidence, assurance, peace, strength, possibilities, and companionship. I now understand what Paul meant in Philippians 4:13, *"For I can do everything through Christ, who gives me strength."*

Fifth, prayer is a means of spiritual nourishment. As much as I need physical nourishment and rest, I need spiritual nourishment more. I need to be spiritually fed and prayer feeds me. Prayer gives enhanced meaning to scripture. It helps me to feed on God's word and believe in his promises and truths.

The spiritual nourishment I receive from prayer is feeding my mind and body. My spiritual being gives significance to my physical being. So often it's just the opposite. How we feel physically and emotionally tends to replicate how we respond as spiritual beings. This should not be so. The more time I spend with God, the stronger I become.

WHY DON'T WE PRAY MORE OFTEN?

God has made Himself accessible to us, yet many believers don't take advantage of the opportunity to speak with God. It takes time and effort to converse with God in prayer. Prayer is an opportunity for us to talk to God. We all have that opportunity and right. However, we can't forget to be still and listen for the other side of the conversation. If this is true, why then is it that so many do not take the time to pray? What is it that keeps us from prayer? I want to share five reasons that contain powerful truths about what keeps us from praying.

The Devil

The first reason is that the devil does not want us to pray, and will invite or create distractions to keep you from it. Prayer is an involvement with God. Prayer is communication with God. Prayer strengthens our relationship with God. Prayer is conversation with God. The devil doesn't like any of this! Prayer allows communion with God and the devil opposes that whole-heartedly.

Prayer will engage various forms of spiritual warfare. Spiritual warfare is a battle between and good and evil. It is a battle between the devil and each of us and our relationship with God. Satan will do anything to neutralize our prayer time because he doesn't want us to be in close communication with God. Remember, we can pray in thought-speak because God can read our minds. The devil however does not have that ability. If the devil is getting in your business with God, you must rebuke or banish him *out loud* and verbally!

Too Busy

Secondly, many of us are just too busy to take the time to pray. From the time we get up until the time that our heads hit the pillow, we are going non-stop. There just aren't enough hours in each day to accomplish all that needs to be done.

We are all busy. That's the plain truth. It doesn't matter how old you are or where you live. Most of us do not wake up in the morning, relax in a chair while sipping our coffee, and ponder what we should do with our day. If anything, we're pounding our coffee while on the run and getting on with our task-filled day.

Each one of our days is filled with an endless number of commitments and obligations, from work, to school, to kids, to chores, to traffic jams and so much more. Yet, I still believe there are moments in our days and weeks where we have "scrap time" and unused moments. This is the time left over after you subtract all your obligations, demands, responsibilities and sleep. Each day, if you deduct the total of all those intermittent "scrap time" hours from your allotted 24-hour day, you will find that most of us will still have chunks of unused time left over. We can decide what to do with those "scrap time" moments and hours.

We all have this time. Think about your life. Not one of us goes 24 hours straight through. There may be times in the day that we daydream, or times we may choose to watch a little baseball or football or our favorite television show. Maybe we may just sit on the couch and watch the news or take a catnap. We all have these moments of choice, not demands.

So often I hear, "I just don't have the time!" I don't buy into that 100%. I agree that our time may be stretched and taken from us by time-consuming whatevers. But there are still moments of choice each and every day to do something we want to do, and to see it as important or something we deserve.

None of us should be so busy that we don't have time for prayer. There is time available to us and we need to take those moments to be men of prayer. Over the past 15 years, I've conducted a series of talks at various churches and camp settings entitled, "Strengthening Today's Family." One of the talks in the series deals with the need of prayer with our family. I have posed a question to my audience regarding prayer and their family. The question is, "How much time do you give to prayer for your family each week?" I spend nearly 30 minutes setting up this question so they understand how to answer it. I ask them to write their answer on a piece of paper and turn it in. All I need is the number—no name or identifying information. How much time each week to you actually spend in prayer for your family?

I then take the average of all the answers. Over the course of all these years, the most common average is three to five minutes. Three to five minutes per *week*. Most of us spend more time watching the news that contains little to uplift us. We actually spend more time watching the commercials during our favorite team's sports event. We even spend more time brushing our teeth or combing our hair. We have got to give more time to prayer and our families and quit being too busy. It is our responsibility to pray for our own family. It is *my* responsibility to pray for *my* children and *my* wife. It's not your responsibility, it's mine. Each one of us needs to take responsibility to pray for our own family. We simply can't afford to be too busy. We all have moments of "scrap time" available to us.

The Place
Another prayer deterrent is focusing our prayer life in association with "the place." Many people focus on *where* they pray rather than the power of the prayer to be heard and answered.

There are many people who have places in their lives where they feel their prayers are more powerful and effective. You've heard people say that at church they feel closer to God, which allows better communication with Him. Some feel that in a church the communication line to God is stronger. Others may feel their communication line is better in the mountains, along the beach, or in a park or cemetery. These are all beautiful places for walking and talking with God. Trust me, I've tried them all!

Unfortunately, we don't spend much time in these places. We don't get to the mountains or the retreats among the pine trees as often as we'd like. The beach and the park are beautiful settings, yet we don't go there frequently. Even at church, most of us will spend from one to four hours a week at a church. Our visit to a church might be once or twice a week.

If we focus the validity and success of prayer on the *place* we pray, our prayer life will be extremely limited. Much (if not most) of our time with God is not spent in these places. These places of worship and being alone with God are wonderful for each one of us and should be encouraged. However, the *place* should not be a restriction for the *prayer*. Our prayers and our relationship with God give meaning to our prayer life. These places are wonderful, yet secondary. We must not allow our absence from these places to keep you from praying.

Skepticism

Skepticism is responsible for keeping many people from praying. Not believing that God is truly listening. Someone once asked me, "Do you really think that God is concerned about me and the things I am dealing with?" There are so many people who truly believe that God doesn't really care about them. Doubt and uncertainty are at the forefront of their prayer life (or lack of a prayer life). I've heard comments like, "It's like I might as well just talk to the ceiling or myself. The words don't seem to be going anywhere. God only converses with important people or very spiritual people and most of us don't see ourselves falling into either category."

When I was young, I attended Catholic Church. I would go to mass on Sunday morning and listen to the priests talk to God. I couldn't understand most of what was being said because it was in Latin, but it appeared to be a special dialogue or prayer language between the Priest and God. When I went to confession, I would confess my sins to the Priest and he would tell me how many prayers to repeat to God, as penance for my sins. When I was eight years old, I wanted to become an altar boy. Something inside of me said I needed to pursue this idea. Now, I had no desire whatsoever to become a priest. The reason I wanted to become an altar boy was because of what I observed taking place during mass. It seemed like all the action and talking to God was taking place at the altar with the priest. I thought, "If I become an altar boy, then I can be at the altar and be able to hear God personally speak." I wanted to participate in the relationship I watched between the Priest and God.

I didn't believe it mattered to God where I was as a person. As a Catholic, my prayers were just memorized words and poems with very little meaning. They truly were not words of conversation and communication between God and me. I didn't believe I mattered to God and that He was listening to me. Why talk to someone when you believe He doesn't want to talk to you? Why would you want to share with Him if you believe what you are saying doesn't matter that much? The priest had the relationship with God, not me.

Another part of Skepticism is wondering if prayer will even make a difference. "What difference is it truly going to make in my situation and with my issues? Come on, just because I am speaking these words to God, what impact is it going to have on me?"

Many people believe that praying is a waste of time and has little influence or effect on anyone's outcome. Someone once told me, "Praying is a waste of breath and time. It's not going to do anything for you. Get off your knees and get on with your life."

How sad that someone could feel this way about prayer and one's relationship with God. Skepticism is a powerful word that can influence one's outlook on life and their character as a person.

Lazy

Last, but not least, as honestly as I can put it, another obstacle that keeps us from prayer is laziness. That's right, being lazy.

Many people don't see prayer as something that's important and needs to be a priority in their life.

Let me share with you some insights into the word and meaning of "lazy". To be lazy means to be disinclined to work at something. Not to want to exert oneself and choose to be active. It implies slow moving. An attitude of getting around to it some other time. Other terms used to describe one who is lazy is apathetic, unconcerned or indifferent. These are powerful words that create a distasteful image of a person.

Many of us can think of people who we feel are lazy at times. Whether at work, at home, or in school—whether it relates to responsibilities or chores—we can identify the word lazy with many situations in life. The one I believe many have to own up to is that they simply don't want to put in the effort. It's just not that high on their priority list, and it's presently not a matter of concern to them. Once again, this is a description of someone who has a lazy attitude towards something.

I have witnessed prayer movements in people's lives and churches. In other cultures, I have read of churches and movements of God, bathed in prayer. Hours devoted to prayer. Rising up early in the morning and praying. Churches filled with people during the week, coming to pray before the sun rises and it's time for work, school and the demands of the day.

Prayer should be identified as a conviction. Effort should be made and time should be devoted to prayer. We must believe in prayer and never be too busy or lazy to devote oneself to it.

In closing this chapter, I'd like to share this story from a friend of mine:

> "I have a nephew who was raised in a Christian home. His dad was a California Highway Patrol Officer. While driving to the store with him and his mom (my sister) one day, the sound of a siren from behind us kept getting louder and louder. We could see the ambulance quickly coming upon us from behind. Of course, we pulled over to let the ambulance go by. The youngster immediately said, "Mom, we need to pray now."

When I asked my sister about my nephew's response, she explained that the siren was a sign that prayer was needed. We prayed for the driver of the ambulance that he could do his job safely and effectively; we prayed for the person(s) who the ambulance was transporting, and for the family of that person(s). We prayed for the doctors and nurses that would be treating that person. We prayed that God would oversee the entire situation and would be with anyone affected by the siren. Being a CHP officer, my brother-in-law was often times the first responder to accidents. When talking to his family about his job, he taught them that they could help him do his job better by praying whenever they heard a siren. I must admit, since that day, I always pray when I hear a siren."

WHAT ABOUT US?

Your Life and Prayer

1. Please take a moment to reflect on the importance and meaning of prayer in your life. When you think of your life and all the roles you play, the challenges that you face, the demands on your life, and the wisdom needed for decisions, just how much is prayer part of your method of operation? How much time did you spend in prayer this past week? Why did you or, more importantly, why didn't you give yourself to prayer?

2. Do you believe in the power of prayer? Do you believe God hears your prayers? Do you believe God listens to your words of prayer that you speak or think?

I'd like to reiterate something about my personal belief in prayer. My prayer time became an intimate communication between God and me. I felt a connection. I believed He did have a concern for me. The more I prayed and believed in prayer, the closer I felt to God. My life and situations mattered to God. I was not on my own. Talk about affirming "Who's Got Your Back," I truly believe God does have my back. I am one of His sheep and part of His flock. God indisputably and intimately cares for Mike Slater.

3. I challenge you to take the time to pray. Come to God in prayer; tell Him from your heart, in your own words, all that is needed and all that you seek from Him. Don't be afraid of saying it correctly. Just talk to your Dad—your Father—your Lord. Speak your words in reverence to God. Speak your words of prayer from your heart. Take time to listen to God responding to your prayers. Don't just say amen and be on your way. Stay for a moment in an attitude of prayer. Let your mind listen for thoughts coming back to you from God. He does and will speak to us. "When trouble beats me up and pounds me down, I shall remain quiet and let God's peace and love roll over me. In God's peace and love, I shall listen and not speak."

As you go on with your day, be aware of God's presence, guidance and involvement within your life and the matters you brought to him in prayer. He will respond to you. Believe in faith of His presence and concern for you and your life.

4. I encourage you right now, to stop for a moment and go to God in prayer. Take a momentary intermission in your day and pray. Just talk to Him and converse in a relationship between you and Him. Whether you're in a restaurant, in a traffic jam, flying in an airplane, or walking through a public place, just take that intermission and reflect on you, God and prayer. You don't have to close your eyes or get on your knees. Just take a moment to stop and pray. He wants to listen to you. He cares.

A Challenge For The Week

Make prayer part of your life. Add it to the routine that makes up your week. As you go from Monday to Sunday, please block out times for prayer. Prayer time can be while you are getting out of bed or taking a shower, while you are fixing your break-fast, while you are driving to work, or when you are riding in an elevator. The nice thing is, there are no rules on prayer. Make prayer a priority and part of your lifestyle. Like they say about exercise, take time three to four times a week to exercise. It's good for your health, your outlook, and your attitude. Well, the same goes for prayer. Make it part of your week. Not just a moment when one feels like they need God. Live it, breathe it and your life will be blessed and strengthened. Keep talking to Him about your situations, what is on your heart. He is listening and will respond.

CHAPTER NINE

IT'S PAST MIDNIGHT
(WHEN ANSWERS NEVER COME)

IT'S PAST MIDNIGHT

For the purpose of this book, my definition of "past midnight" is, "The difficult times and challenges in life that continue and go beyond our reason, resources, strength and our element (estimate) of time."

There are times in our life that are so rough and difficult. They are difficult not only because of the specific issue, but because of how long the issue remains with us and because dealing with the issue is beyond our capabilities and resources. It seems like the issue lingers with us and we feel that there is no change, resolution, or hope in sight. The night gets darker. The darkness represents that issue, and we feel like we are running out of time and hope.

Let me share some phrases and thoughts from people and their life situations. You won't know their exact situations, but you will sense their struggles and despair. These phrases will give you a sense of "past midnight".

> "It never ends. It goes on and on. I pray and pray and no answers seem to come. It is always the same. Always the same. I'm so tired. When will this end?"

> "I'm running out of time. I'm at the end of my rope. I can't go on anymore. I need an answer now."

> "I'm so worn out. There is no more strength left inside of me. I'm tired, so tired."

> "Is it ever going to get better? Am I going to make it, Pastor Mike? I don't feel the answers inside. I'm looking

to you for some answers and some hope. What do you think, am I going to get better?"

"I have the right to be angry. Look at my life and my wife. How much more can we take? How much more suffering? Our prayers are not being answered. Come on, what do you want to tell me that can help?"

"It's so dark and cold. It keeps getting darker and darker. Where is the light? I can't see any hope for this situation."

"It's always the same. It never changes. It just never changes. I'm so tired. We really don't deserve this."

"I don't care anymore. Really, I do not care."

There are times in our lives that can really take a toll on us. There are times that can take a toll not only because of a situation, but the longevity of the matter, and because the answers are beyond our capabilities and reason.

The impact of these moments weighs on us like a thousand-pound weight, affecting us physically, emotionally and spiritually. We carry this weight day-to-day, week-to-week, sometimes for months and even years. It can and does affect many of us. For many, it seems like it's getting closer to midnight, and at midnight, it all can end. That is the witching hour where we can't take anymore. We've come to the end of our rope and feel we are all out of time!

PAST MIDNIGHT—WHERE THE THOUGHT CAME FROM

On Tuesday nights, I teach a home Bible study. I've been teaching it for years. There's a great group of people whom I have grown to love and appreciate in so many ways. The gathering over the years has proven so beneficial not only in studying the Bible, but also in supporting each another. Some churches call these small Bible study groups "life groups", and they truly live up to that name.

The first 30 minutes of each gathering is spent talking, sharing with one another, and supporting each other in prayer and concern. Over the years, the group has grown closer and so transparent and supportive of one another. Following this time of sharing comes the study of the Bible. Because we've been meeting for so long, we have studied *many* of the books of the Bible.

The most recent study was on the book of Psalms. This great book is about a relationship between God and his people. It talks so honestly about life, its struggles, questions that can arise, and the need of hope to continue in life situations.

It seems that no matter what the writer was feeling at times, or how he expressed himself, his difficulties, and his challenges, he always returned to his hope in God. For example, Psalm 56 states, *"When I am afraid, I will trust in you. In God, whose word I praise, in God I trust; I will not be afraid. What can mortal man do to me? Record my lament; list my tears on your scroll. Then my enemies will turn back when I call for help. By this I will know that God is for me. In God, whose word I praise, in God I trust; I will not be afraid. What can man do to me? For you have delivered me from death and my feet from stumbling, that I may walk before God in the light of life."*

Psalm 31 reads, *"But I trust in you, O Lord; I say, you are my God. My times are in your hands; deliver me from my enemies and from those who pursue me. Love the Lord, all his saints! The Lord preserves the faithful, but the proud he pays back in full. Be strong and take heart, all you who hope in the Lord."*

As we continued to study the Psalms for months, many of the group members were relating to struggles and challenges in their lives. The Psalms talk about such times, but also speaks about trusting in God and remaining hopeful in Him. God is aware of everything in our lives and does care about us. The Psalms articulate choices each of us have as it relates to life's challenges and questions. How will it all play out in our lives and how relevant and strong is our belief and relationship to God?

During this time of study, I was experiencing some very difficult and challenging times in my own life. I would rank these challenges as the top five of my existence. It was a difficult time in my career and my future. In all honesty, I didn't feel I deserved all that was happening to me. The answers I wanted were not coming, and the situations continued to drag on. Many who were close to me could not believe all that was happening in my life. Their words to me were, "Everything that's going on with you in your life just doesn't make any sense."

There were times in the Bible study group that I would share some of my challenges. I would express my feeling that I was running out of time and something would have to give soon. It felt like it was 11 p.m. and I only had until midnight for my answers to come. Over the next few months I continued to share with the Bible study group, stating that it now felt like it was 11:30 p.m., getting too close to midnight.

My life and my challenges were similar to a clock. Time was ticking away. I only had so much time allocated to these challenges in my life. Answers and solutions had to come. Prayers had to be answered. Time was ticking away, and it was getting very close to *midnight!*

When my life felt like it was reaching 11:45 p.m., I knew something had to give. I couldn't go on like this. When my Bible study group asked how things were going, my answers remained the same. Nothing was happening. Nothing seemed to be changing and no doors were being opened.

Then I realized something. I had reached the midnight in my life. I had come to the end of what I thought was reasonable and right for my life. I couldn't go on. The situation had not been resolved. The doors I thought would open remained closed. My prayers had not been answered. It now was midnight and there I was with no answers.

As we were sharing in the Bible study group the following week, I admitted that it was past midnight in my life. Never in my wildest imagination had I thought my life would continue to play out this way. I didn't get it. I didn't understand and I couldn't for the life of me figure out why. All I knew was that it was past midnight and nothing had been resolved. What on earth was going on?

In the months to come, my reference to time went way beyond midnight. I would share at times that it felt like it was now 1 a.m.—the wee hours of the morning, yet still so dark. Soon it became 2:30 a.m. Time continued beyond what I expected and thought. The darkness remained as the minutes and hours of my life continued to tick into what I felt was the wee morning hours of darkness—a deep darkness that I was experiencing and had to continue walking through.

IT'S DARK

One thing that I found interesting about the Bible study group and my sharing some of my life's deep challenges was that many people began to identify with the time analogy as it related to some of their issues and dealings with life. Many were dealing with various issues that just seemed to be going on too long. Prayers were not being answered and many were wondering not only why, but how much longer would it be? The weeks turned into months for many, and some were feeling worn out and hopeless inside.

LESSONS AND TRUTHS LEARNED PAST MIDNIGHT

As the minutes and hours ticked past midnight in my life, I began to realize the lessons and truths that were taking place. The truths I was learning proved very valuable and uplifting to me, even in my darkest moments. I began to share these lessons and truths with the Bible study group. Again, as I shared them, many could identify with these truths and could see how they applied to them and their situations. They proved to be of great benefit and hope, not only to me, but also to many others who were part of the study.

I would now like to share with you the lessons I learned past midnight. Lessons learned in the darkness of tough life situations that continued into the darkness, beyond my reason, my resources, my strength and element of time. I pray they will benefit you and your challenging times and will offer hope, strength and truth for living. My prayer is with you at this very moment.

Lesson 1: It Was Still Dark

The first lesson I realized was that it was still dark. Now, this might seem like an obvious observation, but there was so much truth in the statement that I had to accept it and agree with it. It was still dark. It was getting darker. The issues were still there. They did not go away from my life. I did not wake up from a bad dream.

Everything did not magically change like in Cinderella. (I know this may not be the best illustration for a man's book, but you all know the story of Cinderella and what happened at midnight. Just admit it!)

None of the issues went away. I continued to live my days with the same challenges. When asked if anything had been answered in prayer, it still was, "No, not at this moment." It still was dark. The months had passed by and another month was beginning. No way would this month be the same as the previous. Not in my thinking. Yet, it still remained the same. It still was dark beyond my reasoning

Lesson 2: I Was Now Living Beyond My Means and Logic

I had my mind set on just how much I could handle—how much a person could tolerate. I knew my resources and my strength, but wasn't sure if I could endure. I could take so much, go on so just long, and that was it. I had those answers in my mind and I knew I would reach my limit very soon.

I had set the time schedule. I had declared what was midnight. I had given meaning to the situation and the time involved. Maybe I was right on with my time allotment. Maybe it truly was midnight. Time had marched on and it was late in my life. The clock had struck midnight! I was in a deep chasm of darkness and the unknown.

Or maybe my timing was off. What if it was only 11 p.m. and my personal clock was off. Did I misread the hands on the clock? Maybe I was not clearly seeing the exact time because of my emotions, personal thoughts and conclusions. Maybe something else was off. Maybe I couldn't even tell what time it really was. I only knew it felt way past midnight.

I don't know which one it was. I only know I was living beyond my means and logic. I was going on another day, another week, another month. There was strength to continue to endure. There was a flame of faith that continued to burn even though it seemed so dim. I had not thrown in the towel and I did not quit. It was now past midnight, according to me, and somehow I was still dealing with it all.

The questions and challenges remained, yet they were not molding me into something that I didn't want to be. They were not strangling the life breath out of me. Philippians 4:6 reads, *"Do not be anxious about anything, but in everything, by prayer and petition, with thanksgiving, present your requests to God."* The word anxious means to not let any situation strangle the life breath out of you.

One can have concerns and issues in life, but don't let those issues strangle you to a point where you are unable to function. Continue to press on in life. This was happening to me. I was continuing to press on beyond my means and logic. I still didn't quite get it, but not getting it was no longer weighing on me in such a way that I wanted to call it quits.

Lesson 3: I Was Still Here
The thought that I was still here past midnight became a simple yet powerful lesson of hope and strength within me. I was still here. I was facing another week. It now felt past midnight and I was still here. I was still walking. Maybe not that quickly, but I was still moving forward in hope. Maybe my walk looked like a crawl to some. At times it felt like a crawl to me, but it didn't matter. I was still moving forward, whether walking, walking

slowly or just crawling. I was surviving beyond my logic and time element.

The movie *Castaway* starring Tom Hanks clearly portrays these first three lessons. If you can recall, this movie is about a man who is the sole survivor of an airline crash over the Pacific Ocean. The plane encounters terrible weather conditions and is brought down by the storm and crashes into the Pacific Ocean. Tom Hanks survives the crash and escapes from the plane with a life jacket and rubber dingy. He finds his exit through the hole in the plane as it begins to sink into the ocean.

As he swims out of the hole in the plane, he inflates the rubber dingy and it propels him to the surface. Crawling inside of the life raft, he notices parts of the plane on fire in the ocean. He stares at the wreckage and the flames until they all disappear beneath the ocean.

As darkness settles in around him, all he can hear and feel is the rain from the storm. Above him, the only light is that of the lighting from the storm that occasionally comes through the clouds. After awhile, he drifts off to sleep from sheer exhaustion and trauma of the crash. What will await him when he awakes from his sleep? Where will he be, and will there be any hope of survival?

When he awakens, he opens his eyes slowly to the glare of the sun. As he wipes his eyes, he hears the sounds of waves breaking and crashing on a shore. Could that be true? He pulls himself up and peers over the life raft. To his amazement, the life raft had drifted in the night to this island in the middle of the Pacific. He crawls out of the life raft and drags it to the shore. His feet touch land once again and excitement and hope enters his mind and body.

He takes time to investigate the island and call out for help. After days of walking the island and calling out to someone—anyone—he realizes he is the only survivor of the crash and the only inhabitant of the island. He is in the middle of the ocean on a deserted island with no real means of survival. What is he going to do?

In the months that followed, Tom Hanks had to adapt to living on this island. He had to learn how to survive. He had to seek out shelter and food. He discovered how to create fire. Fire for warmth, cooking, and a signal of hope to be rescued. The weeks turn into months and the months turn into years.

Over the whole course of time on the island, Tom Hanks lives out these first three lessons so clearly and vividly. In his logic, it is past midnight. He went beyond the days and weeks he probably thought was possible. Secondly, he was now surviving and living beyond his means and strengths of which he knew. His own resources were being stretched and he was surviving. That thought brings us to the third lesson, that he was still here—still breathing and surviving. Maybe not the strongest, but still surviving way beyond what he thought he could and was capable of. He was the sole castaway, and months later he was still alive! He was surviving.

I WAS NOT MAD AT GOD

As I continued to journey past midnight, I did not get angry with God. This was a powerful truth that gave me comfort, hope and endurance. I was not telling God off and making him the enemy. I did not rant and rave words towards him in anger and frustration. No, I didn't understand what I was going through. I still had moments of why, how come, and what's up? I wondered and questioned at times. I continued to pray and allow God to know how I was feeling and what was going on in my mind.

I continued to be real and honest with God, but I could not and would not get mad at Him because it was past midnight. Finally, so many of the words of the Psalmists became totally understandable. Like David, I was expressing myself honestly and thinking of the situations. I was worn out and felt beat up at times. It seemed like the enemy was winning, yet I continued to draw even closer to God. Like David, I was speaking words of hope and a relationship with God that I truly believed in.

The Lord was my shepherd and I continued to hang on to that truth as I walked through those dark valley times. I cried out to God for hope and strength no matter what time I felt it was. He was walking with me and offering me hope, strength and companionship. Those were three powerful words that were being lived out between God and me.

I had a hope that stayed with me. I continued to believe that everything was going to be okay. This hope continued to give me strength that I know was not of Mike Slater. It was strength beyond my capabilities and character. Most of all, this hope and strength was because of my companionship with God. The word *companionship* became very important and vital to me and my God. We were friends and had a relationship. We were in this together.

Reflecting on a few words from a Bruce Springsteen song, "We were blood brothers in the night, with a vow to remember. No retreat, baby no surrender." A statement that said we would be there for each other. A vow lived out and would not to be broken. This was the relationship and companionship I had with God, even though it was past midnight. I would not be mad at God. He was not the enemy. He was my God and my friend.

THE PROMISES OF GOD

The promises of God, as found in His word, became a personal truth with a deeper meaning past midnight. The promises in the word of God are not just words written in a book. They are truth for living. They offer hope and comfort. They affirm a relationship with God that cannot be broken. They are words that help sustain me yesterday, today, and tomorrow.

The promises of God within His word spoke to me. The key word here was the word 'promise'. By definition, the word promise means, "A declaration that something will or will not be done. An express assurance on which expectation is to be based: an indication of future excellence or achievement. An indication of what might be expected."

A promise is a great truth or thing to have as part of your life. It allows you to feel assurance and expectation. The promises in the word of God began to speak to me with a freshness and assurance for me. I believed not only in the word of God, but the promises of the word of God. Let me share some of the promises that spoke to me.

1. "My grace is sufficient."

2. "The Lord is my shepherd."

3. "I will run and not grow weary."

4. "All things work together for good to those who love and trust in God."

5. "He will make your paths straight."

6. "The peace of God which transcends all understanding will guard your hearts and minds in Christ Jesus"

7. "Ask and it shall be yours, seek and you will find."

8. "Come unto me all you that are weary and heavy laden and I will give you rest."

9. "I can do all things through Christ which strengthens me."

10. "They that wait upon the Lord shall mount up on wings of eagles."

Now that's is a top 10 list that bears repeating! A great list to accept into one's life. I would quote these promises over and over again in my mind. As I pondered these promises, I truly believed that they would come true for me. God would not break His promise to me. I had assurance in these promises and an indication of what was to come. The promises of the word of God became stronger in my life past midnight.

CONTINUED STRENGTH FROM OTHERS

The last truth that became so evident was a continued strength from some people who truly cared for me. So many continued to pray. So many offered resources. So many offered words of encouragement and support. As I journeyed past midnight, so many people made the journey with me. They wanted to see me through. They truly were concerned for me.

I have a drawer full of letters and notes of encouragement from a family who stood with me during this time. Their continued words of love and support have always affected me in a very positive way. Not a month goes by that I don't receive at least two letters from them. There are times when I am compelled to take them out and read them again. The words they wrote remain an inspiration and source of hope, and truly a treasure in my heart.

There's a man who has lunch with me every month. These times of fellowship and support of each other proves beneficial to both of us. We talk, share, laugh and wonder about each other and our challenges. It's nice when you feel you are not alone. I know we will rejoice in the answered prayers for the both of us.

My wife continues to offer companionship and strength during these dark times. She continues to walk alongside of me. She prays for me, and encourages me with her words. Sometimes, her words cut deep with thoughts I need to hear. Sometimes they are hard to accept, but they are always needed. Gilda has been an absolute part of my life for the past 32 years, and for that I am so thankful. Her vow of love and her commitment to me has never been broken or questioned. I am very fortunate to have someone like her in my life. I love you, Gilda!

Because of the strength of those people who continually lifted me, I was not alone in my darkness. To be alone can be a terrible, empty, and hopeless feeling. To wonder if anyone cares about you can be devastating.

To hear and feel someone say, "I am with you," can be so uplifting. To know you are not alone can be a strength that can enable you to continue to press on and face difficult situations and challenges. To know someone has your back is a thought that holds tremendous truth and power. It gives you an advantage.

AN UPDATE

Today is another day in my life. It's way past midnight. I have gone through the early morning hours of darkness. The sun has risen on another day in my life. This day still holds some of the same challenges that brought me to midnight. I wish I could tell you all the challenges have all been faced and conquered. I wish I could tell you that the prayers have all been answered. That would make a great closing to a chapter, but that's just not true!

The truth of this update is that I'm still plugging along. I still believe in the promises of God. I'm living without fear and am not anxious about the situations in my life. They are not choking the life breath out of me.

Yes, there still seems to be some sort of time schedule. However, I'm not caught up in the time schedule. I believe and understand that it *is* possible to make it past midnight. Even though the midnight is dark, God is light. There *is* light in the darkness. I keep on hoping and believing. I truly do believe, "It's going to be alright!'

WHAT ABOUT US?

1. What about you and your life situations? What time is it according to your watch and your timetable? Is it 9:30 p.m. and the clock is ticking forward? Is it 11:30 p.m. and time seems to be running out? It is getting close to midnight? Or maybe you feel that it's past midnight. Do you feel like, "That's it. I am at the end of my rope. My patience and endurance is gone. Enough is enough!"

2. Am I reaching someone today? Even now you may be having serious problems. Are you feeling like you are to the point of despair? Are you finding it hard to sleep and feel that time is running away? Do you feel that sometimes your burden is more than you can bear? Listen. Though you seem to be in the swift current above the falls, you can't imagine how even God could alter things for you. He knows better than you.

3. God is a God of all the time. No matter what time you feel it is. God is not frightened or influenced by time. God is with you even in your darkest hours. God's strength and presence is there, no matter what time it is.

When the road we walk becomes steeper, when the night we endure grows darker, when the load we carry becomes heavier, and when the pain we feel becomes unbearable, God has a song in the night for us. It may be the lyrics set to music. A precious promise from His word that speaks directly to us. A comforting friend who calls out to us or comes by. An insight to help us get through. Or a remembrance from the past. In many ways, God comes to His children in their night seasons with His presence and promise. Can you sense God's presence and promise for you?

4. Make a choice right now to trust God, even if you can't understand the "whys" of what you are going through. No matter what time it is, even if you feel like it's past midnight. It is an act of your will, through faith, and it will enable you to stand firm, regardless of how brutal the storm of life may become.

5. Don't try to figure out how God is going to use adversity for good. Trying to discover His ultimate purpose in such circumstances often leads to absurd conclusions or outright despair. Just trust Him. It really is a matter of trust.

Trust in the Lord with all your heart. Do not lean on your own understanding. In all your ways acknowledge Him and He will make your paths straight.

"No one has ever found their way, who was not first lost." We can make it past midnight!

CHAPTER TEN

WE'RE GOING TO MAKE IT!

THE STORY OF THE FOURTH PLATOON

During my basic training, I was assigned to Charlie Company, Fourth Platoon. There are four platoons in a company, each consisting of 50 men. It is with these 50 men that bonds of unity, development, and support are established.

As a platoon, you eat, train, learn, and sleep as one. From the time you wake up to the time you go to bed, these men are your family and closest companions. Over the weeks of training, you are developed as a unit, working together with a purpose and goal.

During the training, there are times of competition against other platoons. You compete against others for bragging rights or to be the best platoon in the company in some specific area of training. The competition is fierce and all want to win. No one wants to finish second.

I remember weeks into training when we would go on long-distance marches. They were grueling and pushed us beyond what we thought were our limits of conditioning and endurance. Towards the end of the march, platoons would be spread out over a long distance because some soldiers were in better condition than others and many pushed themselves harder than others.

As the soldiers of the various platoons reached their destinations, they would take off their packs, turn and look towards those who had not yet finished. Many would yell out to those still marching to pick the pace and get to the finish line. No platoon could win until all crossed the line.

I recall an incident that took place during one of these marches. Most of us had completed the march with packs and now rested, waiting for the stragglers of the platoon to finish.

There were two heavyset men in our platoon. There was no way they had the physical capacity to keep up with all of us for such a long distance. As they appeared over the hill, words were yelled to them to complete the march and get to the finish line.

As I looked into the distance, the two heavyset men looked as if they were going to faint. Looks of weariness and fatigue were written all over their faces. They continued to struggle on and were the last ones to finish the march. The Fourth Platoon, my platoon, came in last.

The following week we had another march. The picture played out the same. Most of the soldiers finished the march, and then we waited for the two heavyset men to appear and join us. As they came over the hill, I noticed their expressions of desperation. Trying with all they had, they still were losing it as everyone looked on. I turned to my friend and said, "Let's go out there and help them. They need someone by their side right now."

We ran out towards the hill until we reached them, then I told them we were there to help. I asked if we could carry their packs, as that would lift some of the load off of them and make the remainder of the march a little easier. They took off their packs and we put them on. We continued the march together. We went at their pace and talked as friends caring for one another. We finished the march and crossed the line with them.

Later that night, we talked as a platoon about the incident. What took place on that hill at the end of the march stood for something so powerful and taught each one of us a lesson. We came to the conclusion that, as a platoon, we would finish all the marches as one. It didn't matter if we came in first or last, but we had to finish as one. There was the real victory! To finish as one, knowing we would do whatever it took.

During the next two marches, we competed and marched as one. At times, some of the guys in our platoon would be wearing out. We'd come alongside them and say, "Put your hand on my shoulder, it will strengthen you." Some would lift the back of the backpack to lighten the load for a moment. Others would go to the back of the formation so those hurting would not feel like they were the last ones. Words of encouragement were spoken.

At times, the ones in the front would slow down and allow the ones falling behind to catch up. The attitude was, "I will wait for you, and if you have to, wait for me. We're going to make it!"

The proudest moment of the last three marches was when we crossed the line as a platoon. The strongest and the weakest all marching as one. That was a remarkable sight and something wonderful to be part of.

You know, we never won a platoon march. We never came in first. But in the weeks that followed, there was no platoon like the Fourth Platoon. We were 'one' and making a statement to all. In the weeks that followed, people observed and witnessed a group of men, proceeding as one. Many people wanted to be part of the Fourth Platoon but that wasn't possible because you had to stay where you were assigned. I was a fortunate soldier because I was part of the Fourth Platoon.

So many years later, the thought of encouragement and caring for people has remained a vital part of my life and my belief. I have nurtured the thought, grown in it, and lived my life caring for others. I believe that a true friend is someone who is always there when it matters, when it counts, and when it hurts. One who has the ability to reach out to those around you.

Over the years, I have developed a saying that declares so simply and clearly the message of caring for others. The saying is, "We're going to make it." I would like to share with you how that phrase became part of my life and how it has been used to let others know that "I have their back."

THE JET BOUND FOR FLORIDA

I heard a story of an airliner bound for Florida that crashed, that I would like to share with you. In particular, a comment was made at the crash site that has had a tremendous impact on my life. The following is an excerpt from the article that appeared in *Time* magazine:

> Flurries of thick, wet snow swirled through the streets of Washington, clogging traffic and slowing down pedestrians to a labored trudge. As the snow piled up, government offices and private businesses closed early and sent their workers home. By mid-afternoon, traffic on the bridges over the Potomac River that link the capital with its Virginia suburbs had already slowed to a crawl. Meanwhile, Washington National Airport had just reopened after having been shut down by the snowfall for two hours. At 3:59 p.m., a flight bound for Tampa, a Bowing 737 with 74 passengers aboard, began rolling down the airport's main runway for takeoff.

> Lloyd Creger, an administrative assistant in the Justice Department was inching along the northbound span of the 14th Street Bridge in his Chevrolet when he heard the roar of the flight taking off for Florida. He thought nothing of it; hundreds of planes every day take off from National and head out over the bridge.

> But this time it was different. Lloyd watched in horror as the blue and green jetliner suddenly appeared out of the gray mist. The plane slammed into the crowded bridge, smashed five cars and a truck and then skidded into the frozen river. "It was falling from the sky, coming right at me," recalls Lloyd." It hit the bridge and just kept on going like a rock into the water." He remembers that the plane's nose was tilted up when its tail crashed into the bridge, as if the pilot was trying with all his strength to keep the jet aloft.

> For a moment, there was silence and then pandemonium. Commuters watched helplessly as the plane quickly sank beneath the ice flows; only its tail remained visible. A few passengers bobbed to the surface; some

clung numbly to pieces of debris while others screamed desperately for help. Scattered across the ice were pieces of green upholstery, twisted chunks of metal, luggage, a tennis racquet, and a child's shoe. On the bridge, a red flatbed truck with a crane swung over the water. Two of the cars were flattened like tin cans.

Within minutes, sirens began to wail as fire trucks, ambulances and police cars rushed to the scene. A U.S. Park Police helicopter hovered overhead to pluck survivors out of the water. Six were clinging to the plane's tail. Dangling a life preserver ring to them, the chopper began ferrying them to shore. One woman had injured her right arm, so the pilot lowered the copter until its skids touched the water, and his partner scooped her up in his arms.

Then, Priscilla Tirado, grabbed the preserver, but as she was being helped out of the icy river by fellow passenger Joseph Stiley, she lost her grip. Lenny Skutnik, a clerk for the Budget Office who was watching from the shore, plunged into the water and dragged her to land. But the most notable act of heroism was performed by one of the passengers, a balding man in his early 50's. Each time the ring was lowered, he grabbed it and passed it along to another passenger. When the helicopter finally returned to pick him up, he had disappeared beneath the ice.

Meanwhile, rescue workers feverishly tossed ropes and ladders over the frozen river and launched rubber dinghies, but were hampered by floating chunks of ice. As dusk fell, searchlights were switched on, but by 5:30 p.m. officials realized the quest was in vain.

Divers sent down to inspect the fuselage had discovered that nearly all of the passengers were strapped in their seats. The toll; 70 dead, including four motorists. Only five aboard the airplane, four passengers and a stewardess survived the airline crash.

One possible cause of the crash was that the plane's engines might have sucked up slush from the runway, thereby diminishing their power during the critical climb at takeoff. Survivor Joseph Stiley, a passenger on the flight, recalls "the plane was too heavy as it was going down the runway." He remembers turning to his friend in the next seat—who also survived the crash—and saying, "We're not going to make it."

WE'RE NOT GOING TO MAKE IT!

When I read the account of the crash, I remember putting down the magazine and contemplating the content of the article. As I did, I was captured by the phrase that Joseph Stiley had spoken to his friend, "We're not going to make it." I couldn't get that phrase or that thought out of my mind. Imagine hearing those words, and then moments later becoming part of that terrifying phrase. I could not comprehend what his friend must have felt.

It was then that I realized the phrase or thought, "We're not going to make it", is exactly how so many people feel about situations and circumstances that occur in our lives. It may not even be a phrase that sounds so desperate. It could be a statement that bellows frustration. Statements or phrases like, "I can't take it. How much longer? Why doesn't God answer my prayer? Why is this happening to my family or me? It's not fair! It's hopeless. Why me? I'm at the end of my rope. I don't know what else to do."

I began to recall the cries of so many people that I have encountered during my life as a minister. Listening to stories of situations that seemed impossible to solve, challenges people must face, from health issues, financial struggles or divorce to the loss of a loved one. I was hearing from those who were alone, fearful, on the edge, or concerned for what the future might bring. Their dreams had been shattered and their lives upturned. They were not in control of their own destiny. The number of people and stories are so many.

TIME FOR US TO SHOUT

One evening, as I was thinking about the many people who were feeling like they were not going to make it, a powerful thought came to my mind. When people truly feel like they aren't going to make it, our job or ministry is to shout even louder, *"We are going to make it!*

I thought this to be so true and needed. We need to come alongside of hurting people with our voices and efforts, encouraging them, lifting them up, and offering help.

There is a perfect portion of scripture that speaks so clearly to the hurting and their need for someone to come alongside of them to offer help and encouragement. Ecclesiastes 4:9-12 reads: *"Two are better than one because they have a good return for their work: If one falls down, his friend can help him up. But pity the man who falls and has no one to help him up! Also, if two lie down together, they will keep warm. But how can one keep warm alone? Though one may be overpowered, two can defend themselves. A cord of three stands is not quickly broken."*

I believe what the writer is saying is that there will be some pretty tough times in life. Life situations can trip you up and make you fall. It could be of your own doing or maybe the unexpected will come your way and offer you challenges. The writer states he doesn't feel sorry for you that you are faced with this challenge. He does say, *"I pity you for you have fallen and no one is there to help you up."* What is so interesting to me is the word 'pity'. Pity is a word that describes a deep feeling towards someone that is beyond sorry.

He goes on further to say that there are times in life that can be extremely cold. Once again, the reason is not stated, only that the person is going through it. He asks how one can keep warm when you are shivering and freezing within. You can hug yourself, but to no avail.

What is needed during these times is for someone to come beside you with a warm touch of encouragement, support, and their presence. He states that, *"In life, two are better than one."* Though one may be overpowered, put two of us together and there will be the strength beyond one. Put three of us together and there is a cord of three strands that is not quickly broken.

So simply and clearly stated, life brings us challenges to be faced, making us wonder if we are going to make it, and makes us ask, *"how* are we going to make it?" We need someone to come alongside of us to lift and encourage offering strength, determination, resources, hope, and us. We need a stretcher-bearer. A stretcher-bearer shouting *"We are going to make it!"*

SOME STORIES OF SHOUTING

I remember an incident that involved a woman from my church. She was having some medical issues that suggested cancer and possible surgery. I had been informed as to when she would be seen by her doctor to review her test results. I made sure to be there that particular day.

When I arrived, I went to the receptionist to ask if she and her husband had arrived. I was told that they had, and were in consultation at the moment. She asked if I was a family member. I responded, "No, I am her minister." She told me that it would be at least another 20 minutes before the consultation would end and suggested that I take a seat. I found a vacant chair and began to read one of those outdated magazines that are always present in a doctor's office.

After sitting there a few minutes, I had a strong feeling that I was being stared at. I looked up from the magazine to see that the receptionist standing before me. She then asked me "Why are you here? Every week we see 30 or more patients with medical issues, questions that must be answered, and procedures that may be required. I don't recall a minister, rabbi, or priest ever sitting in this office to offer support to a patient. I'm sure many have a church or a place of worship that they attend. So, what brings you here?"

I looked at her and said, "There are times in life when people are faced with challenges and difficult situations. Times when they wonder if they are going to make it. This is such a time for this wife and her husband. I am here to encourage them and let them know that they are going to make it. I can't read the test results or perform the surgery, but I can be by their side to help with prayer and presence, and hope that will be a strength to them at this time."

She looked at me, and after a moment, a few tears rolled down her cheek. The look on her face along with her tears really had an impact on me as I was sitting there. She then spoke these moving words, "Would you tell me about your church? I could use a church like that in my life."

A few moments after our conversation, the door opened from the examining room and the wife and her husband walked out. His eyes caught mine and he walked over to me. We shook hands and told me, "Everything is going to be alright, Pastor Mike. We are so thankful. I want you to know how I felt when I opened the door and saw you sitting there waiting for us. I will never forget this time and the picture in my mind. I'll make you a promise. When people are on that side of the door and I know about it, I will be there for them. No one should experience times like this alone."

I reached out gave him a hug and said, "Way to go!" When people feel like they aren't going to make it, let's shout a little louder, "We *are* gong to make it!" Our voice and presence can make a huge difference in the lives and the challenges that many are facing.

I'M BUYING STOCK IN YOU

I recall a youth conference in the mountains that had a tremendous impact on my thinking, my ministry, and my self worth. Attending this conference as an inexperienced youth minister with my high school youth group, I was in awe of some of the other ministers present...men and women whom I respected and who were an inspiration to me.

One afternoon, one of these ministers came up to me and said, "I would love the privilege of getting together with you Mike. How about meeting me for a soda this evening after I finish speaking?"

I couldn't believe what I just heard. This successful, highly regarded minister wanted to sit down with me and talk. Why? I felt both honored and frightened. Why would he want to take his time and spend it with a youth minister?

That evening we got together over sodas and had a great time getting to know each other. I can't remember all that this man shared with me, but I do remember one statement he made that has stayed with me as a real source of encouragement. It came as our conversation came to a close. He looked me straight in my eyes and said,

"Michael, I want to tell you something. This evening I'm buying stock in you as a person and as a young youth minister. Right now, as you begin your ministry, the stock isn't at a high. But one day, stock in you is going to pay big dividends. I'm buying into it right now, because I believe in you and your response to the plan God has for your life."

Here was a man with years of successful ministry, not yet knowing me intimately, yet willing, not only to sit down and have a soda with me, but also willing to risk himself with words and thoughts of encouragement. He said," I believe in you right now as you begin, even as you experiment and as you grow towards being the man the Lord intends you to be."

That evening, as I walked alone among the pines, I prayed, "Lord, what is this all about? What can the words of this good man mean? Are they words from you? Were they the inspiration and encouragement you know I need to hear? Will the stock pay off and will there be dividends down the road?"

Over and over in my mind I kept hearing the phrase, "I'm buying stock in you now, and one day it is going to pay big dividends...I'm buying stock in you."

If you ask me specifically how many times over the next few years that man called me, I couldn't tell you. If you ask me how many letters and words of encouragement I received, I can't remember. However, the lunches and times spent together over the years were life changing.

A few years ago, this man went to be with the Lord. I gave his wife a call one afternoon and asked if I could pay her a visit. She said she would appreciate that. The following day I went to visit her and found myself sitting at her kitchen table enjoying a piece of cake. She was a great cook and baker. It was during our conversation that I told her that personal story about her husband and me.

When I got to the part about what her husband had said to me, she stopped me from talking. She looked at me with the most tender and peaceful eyes and said, "I know what you're going to say. You were going to say that my husband bought stock in you that evening, were you not?" I shook my head with a tear in my eye. She said, "Michael, I know that story because my husband shared it with me. He believed in you, Michael. He told me, "Honey, God has his hands on that young minister." And years later he told me, "Honey, the stock is paying off.""

Now, many years later, I realize that God placed certain people into my life to be a source of encouragement and support both in my ministry and in my personal life. God really uses encouragers and supporters in the lives of others. Those are the people who shout louder as they come alongside, "We are going to make it!"

WE ARE CALLED TO MINISTER

We are all called to minister. I truly believe that one purpose in our lives is to encourage, lift, assist and help people in some way. When your eyes are focused on Jesus, you awaken to the fact that faith and trust in Christ makes you want to be involved in the encouragement of others.

Remember, it's not just stretcher issues that can destroy people. Often times it's the sense and feeling that no one is there that cares. It's the sense of feeling alone and helpless. Someone once said to me, "I sit alone and wonder, how am I going to deal with this? It is so beyond my means, my ability and me. To whom do I turn?"

I also believe that as we minister to others, God's power will enable us to think, to accomplish and assist in some way. It is written in Ephesians 3:20, *"Now to Him who is able to do immeasurably more than all we ask or imagine, according to His power that is at work within us, to Him be glory in the church and in Jesus Christ throughout all generations for ever and ever."*

A SHOUT OF ENCOURAGEMENT

To those of you who are shouting for help and wondering if you are going to make it, keep your eyes, faith and trust focused on God, not on the circumstances or situations. Do not let time, issues, fear, hopelessness or that sinking feeling get the best of you. It might seem dark at the moment and feel as if time is running out, but don't give into it.

Here are two great scriptures of comfort and truth. *"God will never leave you or forsake you. Come unto me all you that are weak and heavy laden and I will give you rest. Take my yoke upon you and learn from me, for I am gentle and humble in heart and you will find rest for your souls. For my yoke is easy and my burden is light."*

Surround yourself with friends of encouragement; people who want to lift and care for you. Be assured that it is okay to call out for help and assistance. We all go through stretcher times and can use some help.

For those of you who want to shout to others, keep your eyes on Jesus. He will call you to shout and minister to others. You will see and hear (or maybe even feel) opportunities to encourage. You will wake up to the fact that faith in Christ makes you want to be involved in the encouragement of others.

Please remember, God will empower you to minister and assist others. When Jesus calls you into ministry, He empowers you for that distinct ministry and task.

LET'S SHOUT

What sound is coming from you that others can hear? What sounds are coming from your church, week by week regarding ministering to others? We need to become a group of shouters, with voices that speak words of encouragement, assistance and involvement. Voices that are saying, "Even though you think you aren't going to make it, I am here to shout louder, "We are going to make it!"

There is a rare and special quality
in the way some people live.

However busy they may be,
they still have the time to give.

Anything you ask or need,
they will do their very best.

No matter what the task is,
or how simple the request

Kindness just comes naturally
to this rare and selfless few.

Special, giving people
people, just like you!

This spells thanks. Thanks to all who care, lift up and shout.

WHAT ABOUT US?

1. When people feel like they are not going to make it, our ministry is to shout louder, "We are going to make it!" To whom do you need to shout?

2. How can you let your voice and encouragement be known to them?

3. Have there been times in your life when people have come to you expressing words of encouragement and support? What did they do and how did they show support?

4. As you recall these times, would you share one of these experiences with the group?

5. Do you need to hear some shouts coming your way? It's okay to share this need within your group. I pray, if you do, that you will hear the needed shouts of encouragement and support for you.

CHAPTER ELEVEN

CELEBRATION OF COMING HOME

Eleven months and two weeks after landing in Vietnam, I found myself back in the city of Cam Rahn Bay. This was the main city in Vietnam where U.S. commercial jets take off and land, escorting our soldiers who had completed their tours home. I had served my wartime obligation of one year and now I too was going home. I was so fortunate that I had survived without injury. I got my seat assignment along with 200 other soldiers and anxiously headed towards the plane.

The next 24 hours of my life would become one of the most memorable of all times. It was within that 24-hour time period that I would return home from a life-changing journey, set foot once again on the soil of the United States of America, and be reunited with my family and friends.

The last stretch of this 24-hour time period was on a commercial jet from Seattle, Washington, headed back to Los Angeles, California. As I boarded in Seattle, I realized that I would be home in only three hours. For those three hours, I sat there seemingly alone, remembering much of what had taken place in my life over the past two years. I thought about the bus ride to Fort Ord, my first days in the army, and all the months of drills, training and instruction. My thoughts then moved me to the year in Vietnam. My thoughts encompassed so much that happened there, from the moment we landed, to the many battles, military operations and adventures, and the people I became close to that next year of my life. I also recalled the friends and comrades that were lost in various battles. To be honest, the three hours passed by so quickly. I could have used some additional hours to process everything.

As we touched down in Los Angeles, the excitement and emotion I felt inside was indescribable. I wanted to scream and yell out. "I'm home! No more war! No more nights on ambush! No more patrols! No more sleeping in the jungle, wondering if I will make it home." Everything about the war in Vietnam was now behind me. I had served my time honorably, and now I was home!

I was seated near the back of the plane. One by one, the passengers began to exit. They all seemed to take their time, gathering up their personal items and strolling out of the airplane. Finally, it was my turn to stand and walk out. I got up and quietly made my way down the aisle to the door. At the door I thanked the pilots and the stewardesses for their service, then exited the plane.

Then I began the walk up the jet way. As I got to the end of the jet way, just before entering the airport, I could hear a familiar voice. It was the voice of my mom. Her voice seemed to echo down the jet way, with a volume and tone above all the other voices that were speaking. I could hear her saying, "No, that's not him. No, not yet. Still not him." Then came the scream as I entered the airport, "Michael! It's him!" She ran towards me and gave me the best hug and kiss that only a mom could give.

As I looked around, I saw many people that I loved who were there to greet me. My mom and dad, my brother, and many friends. We hugged, kissed and many tears of joy were expressed. They were so happy to see me, but not as happy as I was to see them!

I greeted each one personally. There was no rush to get my baggage and go home. It was a cherished moment that took time to play out. Over the years, I have replayed that event in my thoughts many times. I have only wonderful thoughts whenever I recall my very special homecoming.

Of all the people that came to welcome me home, the one that stood out the most was my dad. After being greeted by my mom, brother and some friends, my dad made his way towards me. He reached out and embraced me with a hug and gave me a kiss. There were tears streaming down his face. It was like a replay of the scene from 12 months ago, and the emotions were just as strong.

It was here, a year ago, that my dad and I had hugged and cried in each other's arms. We had said our good-byes and declared our love for each other. We had played out this scene before. But this time, the emotions, while just as strong, were of joy and thankfulness, and not goodbye. The embrace was one of welcome home; you don't have to leave. We had played out this story again, but now we had a happy ending.

What a moment in my life. So much had taken place in the past 24 hours that I had basically no sleep as I anticipated what was to come. Now, it all came to a climax at the airport. I was now home with my family and friends. What a time of celebration and thankfulness.

WHY DID I MAKE IT?

Why did I make it? Why was I allowed to live out those moments at the airport? That's the ultimate question in a nutshell that I asked myself so many times in the months and years following my return home. How come I made it home? I wasn't gifted nor was I special in any way. Over 58,000 courageous men and women didn't make it home from Vietnam, so why was I so fortunate?

I've given that question a lot of thought over the years and wrestled with what I perceive the answers to be, although I don't fully understand them. I have reached some conclusions that I believe give some insight as to why I made it home. As I recalled the past two years of my life, I realized many of the things that had happened that made it possible for me to return home safely.

First of all, I had trained hard, learned much, and took my responsibility as a soldier very seriously. My life had depended on my skills and how well I used the information I had learned. My training had not been a game, but a matter of life and death.

So much of what I had learned had been played out in real life. My skills and abilities were put into action. They helped me, enabled me, and protected me from harms way many times. I went to Vietnam prepared, and that preparation played a significant role in my return home. And I thank God that I wasn't required to use the knowledge I had regarding prisoners of war!

Secondly, I had taken an honest look at myself. I had to face the fears, doubts and weaknesses that were a part of me. I faced and conquered those feelings. To quit or run away was never an option. I had fought the good fight and run the race as never before.

I grew tremendously as a man, and matured in ways as never before. I gained new understanding of values, conviction, discipline, strength, fear and weakness. All were helpful and beneficial to me.

Thirdly, I was disciplined in what I had learned. Disciplined in such a way that the knowledge stayed with me. I didn't forget what I learned and I followed through appropriately. Day after day, week after week, the knowledge I received during training had become second nature to me.

Fourth was my growing relationship with God. My faith in God proved foundational and powerful. I acknowledged a true belief in the love of God for me, that He truly loved me and I loved Him, and that my love for Him was real and personal.

I learned discipline (or obedience) relating to prayer and the word of God. I talked to God consistently and knew He was listening and would respond to me. Prayer wasn't just a one-way conversation. I shared so much of myself in prayer and asked so much of Him for my life and challenges. Scripture says, *"Come unto the Lord all you who are weak and heavy laden. I will give you rest. Take my yoke upon you. For my burden is light."* Friends, that scripture is pure truth—truth for each one of us.

Reading and believing the Word truly offered me wisdom, comfort and knowledge. I read the Word over and over again and it spoke to me. It was filled with truth for living and comfort and it actually became *"a lamp unto my feet and a light unto my path."*

Lastly, I made it because *we* made it. It was never just me. There were others that were alongside of me that made it possible. There were the soldiers who served with me, helicopter pilots who assisted with supplies, mail and getting us out of the jungle, artillery soldiers who supported our missions, and Air Force jets that were our support as we walked through the jungles. There was also medical staff, intelligence reports that gave us insights into our mission (and thank God for intelligence), and chaplains offering prayers and services for us in the field. The list of support goes on and on. I wouldn't have made it home if it weren't for so many others—some that I met, and many that I never got to meet personally—but they were all there and I knew it for a fact—not a doubt in my mind!

I'd like to share with you a short story about encouragement. I was invited to speak at a gathering of Nazarene pastors on the subject of "Who's Got Your Back" and was given the opportunity to share the truths and beliefs of this teaching in four sessions.

The response and the time together with these pastors were wonderful. I felt a connection and affirmation to the teachings as the day progressed. During the afternoon break, four Armenian pastors approached me. One of them expressed his appreciation and affirmation for this day of learning. He asked me if I knew how the phrase "I've got your back" translates into Armenian. I responded that I had no idea of what the translation would be.

He explained that some clichés or statements do not always translate into another language. However, this was not true of this particular statement. He told me that translation of "I've got your back" in Armenian is "I am your back."

I asked him to repeat that for me. He said, "Mike, the translation means *I am your back*. That means there's no doubt that I'm supporting you. One doesn't even have to wonder or look behind them to see if someone has their back. In the Armenian culture, if you say those words to someone, it's a sure thing. No doubt about it, I am with you, I am your back—you are not alone."

I looked at him and smiled in affirmation. This is what I truly believe and hoped would come across in this teaching—that when those words are spoken, there would be no doubt or hesitation that others truly care and will be there for the other person.

When I began the afternoon session, I shared that conversation. It truly added to the day of teaching and clarified the meaning of the phrase.

I was one of the truly fortunate ones who not only made it home from Vietnam, but also did so without injury. I did my time and I got to board that jet that took me home. So many young men and women did not. I am so grateful to be alive, to have a family and to live in this wonderful country—the land that I love. I thank God that I boarded that plane home with many other young men and women.

CAN THE SAME BE SAID FOR YOU?

As we bring this book to a close, I ask, "Can the same be said for you?" Do you feel that you made it, or are going to make it? Do you feel that your back is covered? This book and its insights are for you. It is intended to encourage you through your journey of life. It is to help you grow as a person in God, and to give you assurance and strength for today, tomorrow, and the rest of your life.

Surviving any war (WWI, WWII, Korea, Vietnam, Afghanistan, or Kuwait) is much like the surviving the wars that are fought within us, for our lives and our souls. There are war zones in our world, whether it is at our jobs, within our families, or in various areas of everyday life. It can be the battle for morals that are pure and holy or it can be battle against pornography. Sometimes it's as uncomplicated as a battle for truth. We hear about these battles every day. Some involve people we know, and others involve strangers that we just hear about. Sometimes, we are the ones at the center of the battles. The fight is on for our loved ones and for us.

Our fight can be as simple as the daily challenges we have to face in life, or can be much more complicated. It doesn't matter how old you are or how young you are, there will always be challenges and times of difficulties you must deal with and face. These challenges can be financial in nature as bills and debt roar viciously at us. It can be relationship problems between a husband and wife, parents and children or among siblings or friends. It can involve rebellion or any of many types of addiction. There are so many battles and wars that must be dealt with.

There is an enemy out there that must be fought and defeated. It can be a spiritual battle with demons working to destroy you and your families. Be aware that there is evil in our midst that wants to devour us. Spiritual battles are being played out regularly.

The enemy can be the world and many of its beliefs. Beliefs that so often are opposed to God and the teachings of the Bible. Just take a look at the world today. Look at what is happening in our schools...and in our government. The lack of values, honesty, and morals should make us realize that we are involved in yet another war.

Be aware that the enemy can also be within us. We wrestle against self-hate, shame, fear, weakness, and pride, to name a few. Sometimes we become our own worst enemy. These things can cause us to self-destruct, and this must not be.

What about you? Do you have any battles or wars that you are currently fighting? Are you in the middle of a battle right now?

I pray this book has helped you in thinking about and discussing your commitment to God, and in helping you to take your faith seriously. I pray you will be committed to others; to support, encourage and truly have their back. I pray this book has energized you to desire a life of purpose, faith, and purity.

REMEMBERING

Since my discharge from the army, several holidays remain very special to me; Memorial Day, Independence Day (July 4th) and

Veteran's Day. They mean more to me than just a time of rest, a barbeque, a three-day weekend or a mini vacation.

Those observed holidays remind me of the time that I served my country. They remind me of the cost of freedom and democracy, and how great this country really is, as well as thankfulness and remembrance to those who gave their lives for our freedom. They remind me of the hurt and pain that so many families have gone through in the past or are going through now because of the sacrifice of a loved one. These holidays remind me to never forget, but always remember, appreciate and take the time to reminisce.

For many of you who read this book as a study with a group of men or women, I encourage you to remember this time of learning and sharing, and to celebrate your journey together. Please, don't just end this 12-week study now that you've finished the book. Make a commitment to get together so you can continue to nurture your newly discovered relationships. Have a barbeque, a Starbuck's coffee, or some type of special gathering to continue your allegiance and support for each another. Gather to remember and celebrate your journey together. Let these gatherings speak to you and strengthen your commitment to each other and your bonds of friendship. We all need special times to remember, so that we can continue to appreciate so many things and grow. Don't let this time of fellowship be forgotten.

MY PRAYER FOR YOU

My prayer for you is that your back will always be covered. That you will know for sure in your darkest hours, that someone has your back. That they *are* your back.

My prayer for you is that you may cover the backs of others. That it will be said of you that you are loyal and trustworthy in the lives of others.

My prayer for you is that you will personally grow in your love for and faith in God. That you will continue to love the Lord with all your heart.

My prayer for you is strength to walk through, endure, and deal with all of life's challenges.

My prayer for you is to trust in the Lord with all your heart. Lean not on your own understanding and He will make your paths straight.

My prayer for you is that you will fight your battles and win; that you will be victorious over the wars and the battles that may come your way.

My prayer for you is celebration—celebration of victories and making it home.

My prayer for you is remembrance. Remember always the good and the positive people and things that have come your way.

My prayer is for you. May God bless you always.

STRETCHER BEARER MINISTRIES

ADDITIONAL RESOURCE MATERIALS

The Book, *The Stretcher* $15

"Becoming A Stretcher Bearer" Self Study Manual $35
Includes workbook and entire seminar on CD

"Becoming A Stretcher Bearer" Audio Series.......................$20
Includes highlights from the seminar on CD

For more resources and to place an order, please visit our website.

SEMINAR INFORMATION

Pastor and author Michael Slater travels the U.S. speaking on the ministry of Support and Encouragement at churches, retreats, colleges, and organizations. For more information on our "Becoming A Stretcher Bearer" seminar or to book Pastor Mike for your next speaking engagement, please visit our website.

CONTACT INFORMATION

P.O. Box 1035
La Habra, California 90633-1035

(714) 869-1440 | mike@stretcherbearerministries.org

www.stretcherbearerministries.org

CPSIA information can be obtained
at www.ICGtesting.com
Printed in the USA
FSOW01n2318120815
9644FS